C000269101

Placing large sibling groups for adoption

**Hilary Saunders and Julie Selwyn
with Eileen Fursland**

Hadley Centre for Adoption and Foster Care Studies,
School for Policy Studies, University of Bristol

Published by
British Association for Adoption & Fostering
(BAAF)
Saffron House
6–10 Kirby Street
London EC1N 8TS
www.baaf.org.uk

Charity registration 275689 (England and Wales) and SC039337
(Scotland)
© Hilary Saunders and Julie Selwyn, 2013

British Library Cataloguing in Publication Data
A catalogue record for this book is available from the British Library

ISBN 978 1 907585 79 1

Project management by Shaila Shah, Director of Publications, BAAF
Designed and typeset by Helen Joubert Design
Printed in Great Britain by the Lavenham Press

All rights reserved. Apart from any fair dealing for the purposes of
research or private study, or criticism or review, as permitted under the
Copyright, Designs and Patents Act 1988, this publication may not be
reproduced, stored in a retrieval system, or transmitted in any form or by
any means, without the prior written permission of the publishers.

The moral right of the authors has been asserted in accordance with the
Copyright, Designs and Patents Act 1988.

BAAF is the leading UK-wide membership organisation for all those
concerned with adoption, fostering and child care issues.

Contents

Acknowledgements

We are very grateful to the Sir Halley Stewart Trust for recognising the need for the research on which this Good Practice Guide is based, and for providing the funding which made the study possible. We also want to express our gratitude to the 37 sibling group adopters and 14 adoption agencies who so generously shared their experiences with us. Finally, we want to thank the members of our advisory group, who offered comments on this Good Practice Guide: Cherilyn Dance (University of Bedfordshire), Lindsay Wright (London Borough of Islington), Jadwiga Ball (Clifton Children's Society), and Sue Dromey (Post-Adoption Centre, London). We also thank Elaine Dibben for her valuable comments on the script. Any errors or deficiencies in this guide are the sole responsibility of the authors and should not be attributed to any of the advisors or the Sir Halley Stewart Trust.

Please note the use of the following abbreviations: VAA = voluntary adoption agency; LA= local authority adoption agency.

Notes about the authors

Julie Selwyn is Professor of Child and Family Social Work and Director of the Hadley Centre for Adoption and Foster Care Studies in the School for Policy Studies, University of Bristol (www.bristol.ac.uk/hadley). Her previous work includes *Adopting Large Sibling Groups* (2011, BAAF), *Pathways to Permanence for Black Asian and Mixed Ethnicity Children* (2010, BAAF), *Costs and Ourcomes of Non-Infant Adoptions* (2006, BAAF), and *Finding Adoptive Families for Black, Asian and Ethnic Minority Children* (2004, NCH).

Hilary Saunders was a Research Associate at the Hadley Centre for Adoption and Foster Care Studies, School for Policy Studies, University of Bristol until 2011. Previously she was the Children's Policy Officer at Women's Aid Federation of England, and she worked for Shelter for 16 years as a policy officer, housing aid co-ordinator, trainer and case worker. Her publications include *Adopting Large Sibling Groups* (2011, BAAF) and *Twenty-Nine Child Homicides: Lessons still to be learnt on domestic violence and child protection* (Women's Aid)

Eileen Fursland is a freelance author. She has written extensively for BAAF as well as for a range of magazines and national newspapers. Eileen's publications for BAAF include *Facing up to Facebook*, *Social Networking and Contact*, *Foster Care and Social Networking*, and a booklet for young people, *Social Networking and You*. Eileen designs and delivers training sessions for local authorities and other organisations around the UK, to help foster carers, adopters and social workers to meet the challenges posed by social networking.

1
Introduction

This guide aims to assist adoption agency staff, children's social workers and other professionals in establishing good practice when they are involved in placing large sibling groups for adoption from the care system. It may also be useful reading for prospective adopters who are thinking of taking three or more siblings.

The guide examines how adoption agency staff and children's social workers handle the adoption process for large sibling groups, with an emphasis on practices and policies which may help or hinder prospective sibling group adopters and the children they wish to adopt. The objective throughout is to give professionals involved in sibling group adoptions clear indications of what constitutes good practice.

Although the guide looks at the decision to place siblings together or separately, it does not focus on the assessment of siblings and their relationships because this has already been covered in *Together or Apart? Assessing brothers and sisters for adoption* (Lord and Borthwick, 2008). Instead it focuses mainly on the recruitment, assessment and preparation of sibling group adopters, linking and matching, introductions, placement, support and the challenges and rewards of adopting a large sibling group.

While some of the recommendations will obviously have resource implications, it should be noted that many beneficial practices simply require a better understanding of what is possible and what is needed. Some aspects of best practice will be similar for all adoptions, but they may be critically important when placing three or more siblings because of the huge emotional, financial and practical commitment required of sibling group adopters. When complex issues could be addressed in various ways, the guide simply highlights factors that need to be considered by adoption agencies.

The guide is based on the findings of a unique study, *Adopting Large Sibling Groups: The experiences of adoption agencies and adopters*, which was undertaken by Hilary Saunders and Julie Selwyn at the Hadley Centre, University of Bristol, from 2009 to 2010, and was published by BAAF in 2011. This was the first study to examine the experiences of adopters parenting a large sibling group, and present the views of social workers engaged in recruiting and supporting such adopters. A key aim of the study was to identify what constitutes good practice in placing large sibling groups for adoption, and the recommendations contained in this guide are largely based on the findings. However, the guide also takes account of other research on siblings, particularly research on siblings in the care system and in adoptive families. Where appropriate, references are also made to the 2011 Adoption Statutory Guidance (ASG) and Adoption National Minimum Standards (NMS), the Adoption Agencies Regulations 2005 (AAR) and the Adoption Support Services Regulations 2005 (ASSR) and *An Action Plan for Adoption: Tackling delay* (published by the Department for Education (DfE) in 2012).

2
Placing siblings together

Siblings matter to each other, whether they share a history or not. After birth mothers, siblings are the next largest group of relatives putting their names on the Adoption Contact Register* in the hope of finding "lost" sisters and brothers (Mullender and Kearn, 1997). Their motivation for searching includes a sense of loss and grief, a notion of the sibling as part of themselves, and just wanting to know if their sibling is all right.

The importance of maintaining sibling relationships is now widely recognised in policy and legislation. However, in practice it can be difficult to meet these obligations and many children end up being placed for adoption away from their brothers and sisters.

Children being adopted today are, on average, three years and 8 months old and often have multiple special needs (Department for Education, 2012). They have usually suffered abuse or neglect, or were born to mothers who misused substances and/or alcohol during pregnancy and/or have a history of mental health problems. Consequently, children's developmental prognosis is often uncertain. Adoptive parenting brings many rewards but also many challenges, especially for those adopting siblings who have different and sometimes competing needs. Attempts to find families for large sibling groups are frequently unsuccessful.

The Adoption Register for England and Wales[†] suggests matches for waiting children with suitable adopters from any part of the country. Although the Register has managed to find suitable matches for many children, they still have difficulty finding adopters for more than two siblings. The Adoption Register 2011/12 annual report shows that in England and Wales, 314 children were referred to the Register for placement in sibling groups of three or more. In that same period, only 25 were placed (seven sibling groups of three children and one sibling group of four), as a result of suggested matches made by the Register.

---

* The Adoption Contact Register enables adoptees and their birth relatives to make contact with each other, after the adoptee reaches age 18 and both parties have registered a wish to be contacted.

† The Adoption Register is a database of children waiting to be adopted and prospective adopters who have been approved; it enables potential matches to be made between children and families.

The expertise of voluntary adoption agencies (VAAs) in placing larger sibling groups is reflected in the fact that all eight of these sibling groups were placed with adopters approved by VAAs. It is not known how many of the 289 siblings were eventually placed together by their local authorities, but it is likely that many were not.

While difficulties in finding a family willing to take a sibling group are recognised, some practitioners question whether LAs do enough to find joint placements for sibling groups. One example is contained in the evidence (Hughes, 2009) submitted to the National Institute for Health and Clinical Excellence to inform the development of guidance aimed at improving the quality of life for looked after children. Having been separated from her six siblings in the care system, Delma Hughes later founded the voluntary organisation Siblings Together. In her evidence statement, she urged social workers to think again and ask themselves if any of the following reasons given for separating siblings in care would be acceptable for separating brothers and sisters living in families in the community:

- 'They fight all the time.'

- 'They are a bad influence on each other.'

- 'This placement is not appropriate to meet his or her needs.'

- 'This placement does not take that type of child.'

- 'We would like to keep them together but there isn't the funding for it.'

- 'We have to focus on the needs of the individual.'

- 'He or she has become too old to stay in this placement.'

- 'He or she needs to be moving on to independence.'

Anecdotal evidence from staff in voluntary adoption agencies also suggests that local authority social workers can sometimes be pessimistic about the chances of finding an adoptive placement for sibling groups, and that this leads to weak and indecisive family-finding efforts.

There is no research specifically looking at the practices and policies that help to create happy and enduring adoptive placements for sibling groups of three children or more. Indeed, there is not a large amount of research into sibling placements in the UK. Studies have focused mainly on the decision-making process, particularly the assessment as to whether siblings should be placed together or apart and the potential benefits and disadvantages of doing so.

The British Association for Adoption and Fostering (BAAF) has published a helpful guide focusing on assessment: *Together or Apart? Assessing brothers and sisters for adoption* (Lord and Borthwick, 2008). While this includes advice on the recruitment, assessment and training of prospective adopters and on introductions, placement and support, it does not explore these issues in depth as its focus is on the assessment of sibling groups needing adoption, nor does it consider these issues from the perspective of adopters and adoption staff. The study was, therefore, the first to examine adopters' experiences of parenting a large sibling group and present the views of staff in adoption agencies who need to recruit and support adopters willing to take large sibling groups.

3

The context
Placing siblings together

LEGISLATION AND STATUTORY GUIDANCE

The law and guidance in the UK are clear that siblings should be placed together if possible and consistent with their welfare, and that contact between siblings should be considered if one or more of them is looked after and placed separately from the others.

In **England and Wales**, an amendment to the Children Act 1989 (S22(c)) states that a placement should enable the child to live together with a sibling. Moreover, Adoption Statutory Guidance (Department for Education, 2011) states that in relation to domestic adoption, siblings should be adopted by the same adopter unless there is good reason why not. Where it is not possible for siblings to be placed together, the agency should consider carefully the need for the children to remain in contact with each other and the need for adoption support:

> *Siblings should be adopted by the same prospective adopter unless there is good reason why they should not be. Where an agency is making a placement decision on two or more children from the same family, it should be based on a comprehensive assessment of the quality of the children's relationship, their individual needs and the likely capacity of the prospective adopter to meet the needs of all the siblings being placed together. Where it is not possible for the siblings to be placed together the agency should consider carefully the need for the children to remain in contact with each other and the need for adoption support ... Where a placement is sought for a child whose sibling(s) have already been adopted, it will be important to consider whether it is possible to place the child with the parents who have already adopted the sibling(s). It must be recognised, however, that this could be placing too great a burden on the adoptive parent, and risk destabilising the existing adoptive family.*

> (ASG 4.12)

In **Scotland**, the Guidance on the Looked After Children (Scotland) Regulations 2009 and the Adoption and Children (Scotland) Act 2007 states:

Local authorities should try to ensure that siblings (children in the same family) are placed together, except where this would not be in one or more of the children's best interests. Where this proves impossible, they should, wherever possible, be placed near each other. The views of each child should be ascertained, as far as is possible given their age and understanding. The regulation uses the term "any other child in the same family" rather than sibling. This highlights the need for awareness of the child's view of 'siblings'. Many families have complex structures with full, half and step siblings and research has shown that children's perception of brothers and sisters and who is in their family is rooted as much in their living experience as biological connectedness.

Where it is not in children's best interests for them to be placed together, or this has proved unachievable, then it may still be appropriate for frequent contact to be maintained. This should be recognised in its own right and not purely as part of contact with parents. Where siblings are placed separately, reunification should be considered at the first and all subsequent reviews, particularly where separation was dictated by a shortfall of placements.

In **Northern Ireland** the legislation in respect of siblings is contained in the Children (Northern Ireland) Order 1995:

Where a Trust provides accommodation for a child they are looking after, they shall, so far as is reasonably practical and consistent with his welfare, secure that –

(a) the accommodation is near his home; and

(b) where the authority is also providing accommodation for a sibling of his, they are accommodated together.

(Article 27[8])

It should be noted that the term "sibling" is not legally defined. It can include step-siblings, half-siblings, or unrelated children who have been brought up together.

On the following pages, we have quoted extensively from guidance published in England, as our research study, on which this good practice guide is based, was carried out in England. However, the focus of this guide is on good practice, and this would apply in all parts of the UK.

ETHNICITY ISSUES

There have been concerns about the disproportionately low number of minority ethnic siblings groups referred to the Adoption Register for England and Wales compared to the number of minority ethnic children referred to be placed singly (BAAF, 2007). The shortage of minority ethnic adopters needs to be addressed locally and nationally, and this may be particularly problematic for half-siblings who have fathers of different ethnicities.

The work of recruiting suitable parents for older children, disabled children, black and minority ethnic (BME) children and children in sibling groups is an ongoing task of adoption agencies. Agencies should make good use of other adoption agencies – local authorities and VAAs – consortia and the Adoption Register, which holds details of prospective adopters who are available and suitable to adopt...

Programmes specifically aimed at developing and sustaining recruitment of prospective adopters from minority ethnic backgrounds will need to be part of the recruitment strategy of the local authority adoption service. Local authorities with small numbers of BME children may well find it a better use of their resources to commission a VAA to find families for these children.

Building and maintaining links with communities, some of which do not have a tradition of parents adopting children unrelated to them, may help to increase the number of prospective adopters from a wide range of minority ethnic backgrounds. The importance of increasing the recruitment of BME prospective adopters is underlined by Selwyn et al (2008). Their study of the care pathways of white and BME children showed that age and ethnicity are the two major determinants of adoptive placements. BME children had fewer prospective adopters showing interest in them and, if no placement could be found, their plans tended to be changed away from adoption at an earlier point than for their white counterparts.

(ASG 3.11–3.13)

Ethnicity may be a consideration in matching, but the Government's plans for adoption reform make it clear that failing to match children with adopters because they are of a different ethnicity is unacceptable:

Where there are two sets of suitable parents available then those with a similar ethnicity to the child may be the better match for the child. Sometimes an ethnic match will be in a child's best interests, for example, where an older child expresses strong wishes. However, it is not in the best interests of children for social workers to introduce any delay at all into the adoption process in the search for a perfect or even partial ethnic match when parents who are otherwise suitable are available and able to provide a loving and caring home for the child.

An Action Plan for Adoption: Tackling delay (DfE, 2012), para 52

In Scotland, the Looked After Children (Scotland) Regulations 2009 state the following:

Some particular dilemmas that arise concern the priority given to seeking a family who will meet the cultural needs of a child, especially one which actively reflects a child's ethnicity and/or religion. Staff involved in this area of work should keep up to date with current research on the experiences of adopted people who grow up within families who do not share their ethnicity and the current profile of adopters in their area and across Scotland. These will inform decisions about how long should be given before considering adopters who may not fully reflect a child's culture but who have identified strengths in supporting a child from a different background. Racial, Cultural and religious background should not be a barrier or delay in placing children in stable and secure permanent placements as early as possible...

Throughout the regulations, as in the legislation, there is reference in different forms to the religious persuasion of the child and parents, including any details of any ceremonies pertinent to that religion, as well as their ethnicity, culture and any linguistic needs. This should form an important part of articulating the child's needs in seeking an adoptive placement. However it should not form a barrier to a placement suitable on other grounds.

AVOIDING DELAY

Adoption agencies in England should generally adhere to the timescales set out in the Adoption Statutory Guidance, unless the agency considers that in a particular case this would not be in the child's interests. Where the agency is unable to comply with a timescale or decides not to, it should record the reasons on the child's case record. The paramount consideration must always be the welfare of the child.

Deciding if a child should be placed for adoption

The timescales set out below apply to all adoptions in England:

The child's need for a permanent home should be addressed and a permanence plan made at the four month review;

The adoption panel should receive all necessary information from the agency within six weeks of the completion of the child's permanence report (CPR); and

The adoption panel's recommendation on whether the child should be placed for adoption should be made within two months of a review where adoption has been identified as the permanence plan.

Where the agency is unable to comply with a timescale or decides not to, it should record the reasons on the child's case record.

(ASG 2.2)

Treatment of prospective adopters

Written information about the adoption process should be sent within five working days to the enquirers in response to their enquiry;

The enquirers should be invited to an adoption information meeting or be offered an individual interview by the agency within two months of their enquiry;

The adoption panel should receive all necessary information about the prospective adopter from the agency within six weeks of the completion of the prospective adopter's report; and

The adoption panel's recommendation about the suitability of the prospective adopter to adopt a child should be made within eight months of the receipt of their formal application.

(ASG 3.1)

Placing a child with a prospective adoptive family

A proposed placement with a suitable prospective adopter should be identified and approved by the adoption panel within six months of the agency deciding that the child should be placed for adoption;

Where a birth parent has requested that a child aged under six months be placed for adoption, a proposed placement with a suitable prospective adopter should be identified and approved by the panel within three months of the agency deciding that the child should be placed for adoption.

(ASG 4.1)

In Scotland, a current focus on achieving permanence, including adoption, has resulted in local authorities actively reviewing care planning processes and timescales and seeking to maximise the use of Scotland's Adoption Register and other locally based resource-sharing services. The Guidance on the Looked After Children (Scotland)

Regulations 2009 and the Adoption and Children (Scotland) Act states the following:

> Where the agency may have difficulties in identifying adopters who could meet a child's needs arising from their religion, culture, ethnicity or any other needs the panel recommendation should highlight this so that the Agency Decision Maker can authorise the resources for a search for an appropriate family beyond the local authority's own resources. There are many options for this in the different resource sharing mechanisms established to link children with approved families through local consortia, across Scotland and also UK wide. Some adoption agencies might also wish to consider specific recruitment initiatives. This should be identified and acted upon early **so that there is no undue delay** for the child. It should be remembered that research has shown that a stable, secure placement found early in a child's life is more important to their welfare than delaying for a "prefect" match.

NEW "ADOPTION SCORECARDS"

Adoption scorecards were introduced as part of a new approach to address delays in the adoption system, set out in *An Action Plan for Adoption: Tackling delay* (published in March 2012).

> The Government will ... publish new adoption scorecards for each local authority, which will then be updated annually when new data become available. The scorecards will highlight key indicators for how swiftly local authorities place children in need of adoption and how swiftly they and adoption agencies deal with prospective adopters. They will allow local authorities and other adoption agencies to monitor their own performance and compare it with that of others.

(Para 97)

However, speed is not the only consideration, and the "scorecards" take into account the reality that some children are harder to place:

> We don't want it to distort local authority decisions about whether adoption is the best option for children, for example, by discouraging them from placing some children for adoption – such as older children, those in sibling groups or those with complex needs. Both the Department, in looking at local authority performance in relation to the scorecards, and Ofsted in their inspections, will take account of and give credit to local authority efforts to place children for whom it is difficult to find a family.

(Para 102)

Adoption Scorecards are still current and have already been updated once (in November 2012, with a further update due in autumn 2013). The original published scorecards and the November 2012 updates are both available to download from: www.education.gov.uk/childrenandyoungpeople/families/adoption/a00208817/adoption-scorecards.

Some parts of the data (e.g. on prospective adopters) are still not available but the scorecards state that they are due to be published in 2013.

THE ADOPTION REGISTER AND THE INTER-AGENCY FEE

When the child's LA cannot find suitable adopters from their own pool of prospective adoptive families, they may widen the search and find adopters through a voluntary adoption agency or another LA or a consortium – and when this happens, the child's LA has to pay an "inter-agency fee" to the VAA or LA that approved the adopters.

The chances of a child not being adopted nearly double with each year of delay (Selwyn *et al*, 2006), but adoption agencies can reduce delay by being willing to pay the inter-agency fee required for a VAA placement and having sufficient funding to do so:

Agencies are required to refer children to the Adoption Register when they are not actively considering a local match for the child, i.e. being in the process of exploring a potential match with a named prospective adopter. Referrals can be made either when the agency's decision maker has decided that the child should be placed for adoption or after three months of that decision during which the agency had unsuccessfully sought a local or consortium match. If legal proceedings are ongoing at this stage, and the child is subject to an interim care order, referral to the Adoption Register can be made provided the necessary consents and the court's agreement have been obtained.

(ASG 2.71)

Where a local authority is aware that a particular prospective adopter approved by another adoption agency can best meet the needs of a child, they should negotiate with the agency about the possible placement of the child with that family. Unwillingness to pay an inter-agency fee should not be the reason for not placing the child. Indeed, Selwyn J's research, Adoption and the Inter-agency Fee, *provides clear evidence that effective use of VAAs has a positive impact on finding suitable and timely placements at a lower cost for local authorities. It shows that local authorities have under-estimated their own costs and that this has influenced their belief about the costs of VAA placements: the true costs of both VAA and local authority family finding are almost identical at around £36,000, which is similar to the cost of the child remaining in foster care for 18 months. The research found that where adoption is the right option for a child, a timely adoptive placement could save approximately £25,000 for each subsequent year, after the first, that the child is not in care.*

(ASG 4.19)

As outlined above, statutory guidance already requires local authorities to refer to the Adoption Register all children for whom they do not identify a potential family within three months of the decision that adoption is the best plan for them. *An Action Plan for Adoption: Tackling delay* (Department for Education, 2012) proposes that the Government make this requirement in regulations. Local authorities should, of course, continue their own direct efforts to search for suitable families in parallel. It also proposes a legislative requirement on all adoption agencies to refer to the Adoption Register all prospective adopters who are not being matched to a child within three months of being approved (provided the adopters agree). A further proposal in the Children and Families Bill aims to enable prospective adopters to directly interrogate the Register.

Adoption agencies can implement some of these proposals immediately within the existing regulatory framework, but significant changes should be anticipated for 2013/14.

It also intends to review the effectiveness of local authority commissioning arrangements for adoption, and to consider whether further action should be taken to increase the role of voluntary adoption agencies in the system.

An Action Plan for Adoption: Tackling delay (DfE, 2012) includes this interesting solution to the challenge of finding funding to pay for placements by VAAs:

One innovative proposal that may have the potential to address this issue is a social impact bond under development by the Consortium of Voluntary Adoption Agencies. It could make a significant difference by releasing the necessary funding to allow voluntary adoption agencies to find prospective adopters for children with the most severe and complex needs through intensive marketing and recruitment and by offering high levels of expert adoption support.

(Para 87)

Scotland's Adoption Register, developed in the last two years, now provides a unique Scotland-wide child and family linking service. Funded by Scottish Government, the Register maintains a database of children awaiting placement and available families. The Register also arranges exchange days and film evenings at which prospective adopters have the opportunity to see information on children awaiting placement.

In Northern Ireland, the Adoption Regional Information System – ARIS – is a similar database that stores details of children waiting for adoption and approved adopters in Northern Ireland to improve the chances of children finding an adoptive family by suggesting links where agencies have not been able to place children locally with a suitable family.

ADOPTION SUPPORT

The variation in support services provided to adopters and adopted children may be due to a lack of clarity in the legislation and regulations on adoption support. Under the 2002 Adoption and Children Act (s.2(6)), adoption support services are defined as counselling, advice and information and any other services prescribed by regulations. The 2011 Adoption Statutory Guidance (Chapter 9) contains a table headed 'People to whom adoption support services must be extended: ASR 4', which sets out the various services for which an agency adoptive child and his/her adoptive parents are 'entitled to be assessed'. However, this is qualified by the following statement:

> ASR 4 sets out the persons to whom the local authority must extend adoption support services. That is not to say that every service must be supplied to each person in the category, rather that the local authority is obliged to ensure that these services can be made available if an assessment shows that they are needed.

(ASG 9.6)

These words are clearly intended to protect LA budgets from being overwhelmed by excessive demands. However, they also absolve LAs from the obligation to provide the support assessed as necessary for individual families. This is a dangerous loophole, because LAs looking for ways to cut budgets may be less willing to provide adoption allowances and support services – and the lack of adequate support could severely limit the chances of large sibling groups being adopted.

However, in a new initiative in England, First4Adoption and the Department for Education have published a new guide to the support available for people who have adopted a child. It brings together the latest information about the entitlements and support that may be available for adoptive parents and their children. It also includes information about the proposed changes to Statutory Adoption Pay. The "adoption passport" guide aims to give adopters information about the kinds of post-adoption support that may be available from their local authority, such as access to counselling and training to help adopters meet the needs of their adoptive child; financial support; priority access to social housing; and social activities for adoptive families. It also gives information about the Government's plans to change adoption leave and adoption pay entitlements to bring them more into line with those offered to biological parents. This includes the right to take time off in the earlier stages of the process, when prospective adopters are meeting their child, before they move in. There is also information about getting priority access to schools for an adopted child and the latest plans to offer free early education for adopted children from the age of two.

In Scotland, the Adoption Support Services and Allowances (Scotland) Regulations 2009 state what is available and what adopters can expect:

All current prospective adopters should receive information about their right to request an assessment. Any adopters with whom the agency has contact who have completed the legal adoption and who qualify as a 'relevant family' should also receive this information. Once a local authority has procedures in place for assessing adoption support needs and has audited their adoption support services they should consider, as part of their adoption services plan, how they will inform families of this provision...

The 2007 Act lists in section 1(5) as the meaning of adoption support services the provision of counselling, guidance and 'any other assistance in relation to the adoption process that the local authority providing an adoption service in a particular case considers appropriate in the circumstances of that case'. The regulations provide more details about use of adoption allowances and the range of financial support that may be made available but does not further define the nature of services that may be considered. This allows scope on one hand for creativity in developing services but carries the risk of patchy development across Scotland and a lack of clarity about what adopters can expect.

4

Research on large sibling groups: a brief overview

There is a considerable body of research on siblings but much less on large sibling groups. The findings from studies on sibling pairs may not be valid for larger sibling groups. Most of the available literature on the adoption of large sibling groups consists of practitioners' reflections on a few cases or recommendations for practice. It can also be difficult to assess the outcomes of sibling adoptions, because sibling studies often consider fostering and adoption together (e.g. Rushton *et al*, 2001; Hegar, 2005), include sibling groups under the heading of 'special needs adoptions' (e.g. Rosenthal *et al*, 1988; McRoy, 1999) or compare sibling placements with those of single children as well as single separated siblings (e.g. Boer *et al*, 1994; Rushton *et al*, 2001).

Sibling relationships

Siblings who grow up together have an important influence on each other, because children understand their siblings so well and feel very strongly about them (Dunn, 1984). Sibling relationships can be an integral part of a child's sense of identity, while potentially providing support, companionship, continuity, competition and conflict (Edwards *et al*, 2006). Children can develop strong bonds with their siblings, especially when they are involved in caring for them (Dunn, 1993). Intense sibling loyalties tend to exist where the parents have been weak, absent, hostile or have died during the siblings' formative years (Bank and Kahn, 1982).

Being adopted with siblings

A survey (Ivaldi, 2000) found that over half (56%) of adopted children in 116 local authorities in England in 1998/99 had two or more siblings and 24 per cent had one sibling, but nearly two-thirds (63%) of the children were placed singly and placements of three or more siblings accounted for only seven per cent of the sample.

Being placed together or apart

A survey of adoption agencies in England and Wales (Dance *et al*, 2010) found that the proportion of children placed with a sibling varied by LA from 14 per cent to 80 per cent of placed children. This suggests differential policies on the separation of siblings and the speed with which children are removed and placed for adoption. Siblings are most likely to be separated when entering or leaving care (Kosonen, 1996). If children are placed singly, it is often because they have more severe personal problems (Rushton *et al*, 2001), which inevitably impacts on outcomes (see below).

Greater chance of adoption for sibling groups in the US

Contrary to common assumptions in the UK, a large-scale study of children photolisted for adoption in the United States (Avery and Butler, 2001) found that belonging to a sibling group requiring a joint placement for adoption *increased* the probability of adoption, and each additional child in the sibling group speeded up adoption by approximately 3.2 months. Featuring children repeatedly brought a diminishing response, so the researchers suggested that, after updating the profile twice, paying a specialist agency to find suitable adopters would probably be more successful.

Outcomes of sibling placements

An overview (Hegar, 2005) of 17 studies on siblings in foster care or adoption concluded that 'joint sibling placements are as stable as or more stable than placements of single children or separated siblings, and several studies suggest that children do as well or better when placed with their brothers and sisters'. If separated and placed singly, children had an increased risk of poor outcomes (Fratter *et al*, 1991; Quinton *et al*, 1998; Leathers, 2005), but often children were placed singly because they had more severe problems (Rushton *et al*, 2001).

Outcomes with birth children

The presence of birth children in the family has been associated with higher disruption rates for sibling adoptions (Boneh, 1979; Wedge and Mantel, 1991; McRoy, 1999), but Wedge and Mantel found no disruptions when the adopted children were at least three years younger than the youngest birth sibling.

Conflict with siblings

The narrower the age gap, the more likely it is for there to be conflict between siblings but also more closeness, especially with same-sex siblings (Furman and Buhrmester, 1985). As sibling conflict may destabilise an adoptive placement (Rushton *et al* 2001), this needs to be considered when preparing and supporting sibling group adopters (assuming that assessment has concluded that joint placement is appropriate). Fortunately, the intensity and frequency of negative interactions between siblings usually decrease as children grow older (Buhrmester and Furman, 1990; Kim *et al*, 2006).

Contact with siblings

In one study (Rushton *et al*, 2001) of siblings in foster care and adoption, half of the placements were made without any plan for sibling contact, although contact was viewed positively by the families and had positive outcomes. Over two-thirds of adult adoptees who had direct contact with birth relatives formed the closest relationship with their siblings (Triseliotis *et al*, 2005).

Joint sibling placements as a protective factor

Placing siblings together appears to offer protection in situations where difficulties might be expected. Children rejected by their birth parents tend to have poor outcomes (Quinton *et al*, 1998), but not if they are placed with their siblings (Rushton *et al*, 2001). Similarly, older children often have poorer outcomes in adoption than children who are placed at a younger age, but a study of international adoption outcomes after 10 years (Boer *et al*, 1994) found that, although children adopted with siblings were on average older at arrival, they did not in general have higher problem scores and a higher disruption rate. It is important to note that research has consistently found that adoption is more stable than foster care (Triseliotis, 2002; Biehal, 2010).

5

Our research: aims, sample and method

AIMS

Our study aimed to understand more about: a) the experience of adopting a large sibling group from the perspective of the adoptive parents and b) the experience of social workers in recruiting, preparing and supporting such adopters. Specifically the study explored the motivation of sibling group adopters, variations in the practice of adoption agencies, the experiences of the adopters and the rewards and challenges of adopting a large sibling group. It is the only such study that considers the experiences of adopters parenting large sibling groups.

THE SAMPLE

Fourteen adoption agencies – five local authority adoption teams (LAs) and nine voluntary adoption agencies (VAAs) – were recruited to participate in the study. All had had three or more siblings placed with their adopters in recent years. Sibling group placements comprised two – ten per cent of all adoptive placements in these agencies. To recruit adoptive parents, the 14 agencies sent out letters to adopters who had taken a large sibling group, inviting them to take part in the study. Publicity through Adoption UK also elicited responses from other sibling group adopters. The final sample of 37 sibling group adopters came from England, Wales and the Isle of Man; 20 had been approved by a VAA and 17 by an LA. These families had a total of 119 children and young people placed with them: 30 groups of three siblings, six groups of four and one group of five. One family had eight children, having adopted a second group of four siblings.

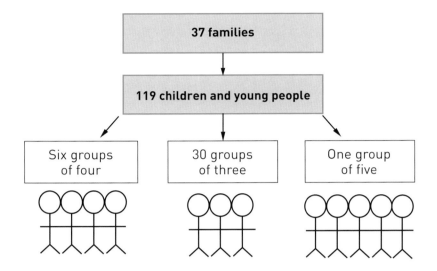

METHODOLOGY

Face-to-face semi-structured interviews were conducted with adoption managers and social workers in the LAs and VAAs and with the sibling group adopters. The interviews looked at the whole adoption process and explored agency practices and the experiences of the adopters, including what they found helpful and unhelpful. All the adopters completed the General Health Questionnaire (GHQ28) and also a Strengths and Difficulties Questionnaire (SDQ) (see www.sdqinfo.com) on each of their children. Quantitative data were analysed in SPSS and qualitative data using a framework approach in NVivo.

6

The characteristics of the siblings and their adopters

THE CHILDREN

The 119 children placed with sibling group adopters in our sample included 70 girls and 49 boys and five sets of twins. All of the children were white. The average age at placement was four years and five months, and in four sibling groups all the children were under age five when placed. Most siblings were narrowly spaced in age, having been born within 10–12 months of each other. Most (26) of the sibling groups were a mix of boys and girls, but there were nine all-female groups and two all-male groups.

The preponderance of girls may reflect a belief, acknowledged by one adopter, that girls would be "easier to manage". Seven out of the ten twins were male and research (McKay, 2010) shows that male twins in particular are at greater risk of becoming looked after.

Some adoption social workers thought it was unrealistic to expect adopters to take on three or more siblings under school age. Often this concern was expressed in the rhetorical question: 'How many hands does one person have?' The adopters sometimes found practical solutions to this problem, such as preparing lots of meals and storing them in the freezer before the children were placed; placing child safety gates on every door, and training the oldest child to walk beside the buggy containing the two younger children holding onto the side bar. However, two of these adopters found that trying to meet the needs of three very young and troubled children was an overwhelming task.

Sixteen children (13 per cent) were described as having learning difficulties, and many others needed to catch up on missed education.

All the children had been placed with two parents, including one female same-sex couple. The average age of adoptive mothers was 41 years old, and for fathers 42. In three of the 37 families, the adoptive father was the main carer. Only two of the families had previous experience of parenting before the sibling group was placed.

Nearly all of the children were placed with childless couples. Some adoption managers expressed the view that placing a sibling group with adopters who already had birth children would be too risky. However, two LA managers who were prepared to consider this emphasised that the birth children had to be fully involved in the assessment. A social worker also described how *adult* children had provided support for their parents, when they adopted a large sibling group.

Almost half of the siblings had been living in separate foster homes before being re-united in adoption. This suggests that LAs have considerable difficulty in finding foster carers for large sibling groups.

The children were placed with their adoptive families on average a year later than most adopted children in England. Siblings placed with a VAA adopter were also significantly older than those placed with an LA adopter – probably due to a tendency amongst LAs to use VAAs only as a last resort. (One manager acknowledged that her LA did not always have enough funds to pay the inter-agency fee for a VAA placement.)

THE ADOPTERS

All the sibling group adopters were white. Apart from having a large enough house and garden, key characteristics of the adopters in our sample were their determination to adopt a sibling group and their commitment to making the placement a success. Many had a great deal of confidence and belief in their own judgement and were not afraid to challenge professionals to ensure that their children received the necessary support.

Some of the ways in which they signalled their determination to be taken seriously and to make the placement work included: insisting that the local authority should recognise the child's needs and pay for therapy or learning support; refusing to apply for the adoption order until the necessary support was provided; threatening to pull out if there was any more delay; insisting that it was "all or nothing" when social workers wanted to split the siblings; and making formal complaints and taking legal action against the children's LA.

One VAA manager suggested that sibling group adopters have the following qualities:

> *...an ability to really ask questions and the ability to say, 'You haven't given me the answers that I need to have, before I make my decision'... They're pushy people, so they will be good advocates for kids, and they drive you crazy because they are! I'd much rather have them as adopters than people who actually don't do that.*

PRACTICE IMPLICATIONS

- **Sibling conflict needs to be considered when preparing and supporting sibling group adopters**, especially when there are narrow age gaps between the children. When there are high levels of sibling conflict, therapeutic intervention may be needed before or after the children are placed. Multi-agency work to ensure the provision of learning support should take place before placement.

- As it can be difficult to re-unite siblings who have lived apart for a considerable time, **LA managers urgently need to consider ways of attracting suitable foster carers for large sibling groups** and of working positively with separated siblings. If siblings cannot all be fostered together, ideally they should be placed and should remain with a sibling with whom they get on well. It also helps if they can live in the same area, attend the same school and have frequent contact.

- **The delay in placing the sibling groups indicates a need to improve the social work and legal systems** to enable social workers to complete the necessary assessments and paperwork more quickly and to reduce delays in legal proceedings. LAs can also reduce delay by referring cases to the Adoption Register and having sufficient funds to pay the inter-agency fee.

- **It would appear that adoption staff are understandably wary of placing three or more siblings** into a household where children are already living, given the risks identified by research. However, it should be noted that Wedge and Mantel (1991) found no disruptions when the adopted children were at least three years younger that the youngest birth sibling.

- Our findings suggest that whenever three or more siblings under the age of five are being placed for adoption, **the LA needs to provide home help right from the start.**

- **The shortage of minority ethnic adopters may be particularly problematic for siblings who have fathers of different ethnicities.** This issue needs to be addressed locally and nationally. Agencies need to develop recruitment strategies targeted at BME communities, as well as work collaboratively with other agencies to recruit adoptive parents.

7

Keeping siblings together

DECISION-MAKING

The decision to separate or keep siblings together was made by social workers and managers in the children's local authority, often in conjunction with the courts. This decision was not the responsibility of voluntary adoption agencies (VAAs). Respondents in the five local authorities (LAs) participating in our study were asked how decisions were made to separate siblings or to keep them together, and about the factors that influenced those decisions.

LA staff were reluctant to separate siblings with adoption plans, and decisions to do so had to be well-evidenced. Decisions were generally made in a permanency planning meeting involving the children's social worker, the team manager and a senior member of the adoption team. Sibling group issues were also discussed by adoption panels and at Looked After Children (LAC) reviews.

Courts and children's guardians were thought to have a considerable influence on decisions involving siblings. Sometimes local courts opposed the adoption plan. Two LA managers expressed frustration that difficulties in placing sibling groups were compounded by delays in legal proceedings. They attributed these problems to recent changes in the legislation on adoption and the insecurity of care orders and placement orders (as opposed to freeing orders) that were contested by the parents. A number of factors influenced the decision to keep siblings together or separate them. Assessments of the children sometimes recommended that their individual needs were so great that it would be preferable to separate them. Attachment difficulties or sexual abuse between siblings were sometimes seen as contra-indications to keeping the group together. However, difficulty in finding suitable adopters was the most frequent concern.

LA managers said that usually three to six months were spent searching for suitable adopters and if the search proved fruitless, social workers would have to decide whether to go on searching or to look for the most practical alternative placement.

Social work staff acknowledged that their strong belief that siblings should be kept together often had to give way when no suitable adopters could be found. Pressure to split the group increased as time moved on.

Some LA managers thought that social workers sometimes found it difficult to manage the strong emotions that tended to accompany the separation of siblings, and that avoiding a difficult decision could contribute to delay in some cases.

OVERCOMING THE BARRIERS

Agency staff stated that barriers to placing large sibling groups together in foster care or for adoption included:

- difficulties in finding foster carers for large sibling groups;
- relatives wanting to separate siblings with different fathers;
- delays in court proceedings;
- a shortage of adopters willing to take three or more siblings;
- inadequate funds to pay the inter-agency fee required for a placement with another agency; and
- concerns that adopters would be overwhelmed by the children's needs.

Placing a large sibling group for adoption was also said to be time-consuming, because the necessary paperwork and assessment had to be completed for each child. One manager spoke about having to resist concerns about delay, as that could result in pressure to place the siblings separately.

A SHORTAGE OF ADOPTERS FOR LARGE SIBLING GROUPS

With regard to the perceived shortage of willing adopters for large sibling groups, *An Action Plan for Adoption: Tackling delay* (DfE, 2012) states:

> *We do not have comprehensive national data comparing the number of approved adopters with the number of children in need of adoption, but the numbers from the Adoption Register give the best available indication. The Register accounts for around 12% of matches each year, and referrals to it are not consistent across adoption agencies. Nevertheless, it is worth noting that there are currently around 2,000 children on the Register because a family cannot be found for them*

locally, but only 325 approved adopters. There are about 80 sibling groups of three on the Register, and only about three adopters willing to consider adopting up to three children.

Are some prospective adopters being given fewer children than they want?

Perhaps things have changed in recent years. Interestingly, in 2000 Ivaldi found that although five per cent of prospective adopters were prepared to accept a group of three or more siblings, over half of these adopters eventually had just a single child or a sibling pair placed with them. The remaining adopters went on to adopt groups of three, four or five siblings (Ivaldi, 2000).

PRACTICE IMPLICATIONS

Our findings suggest that LA managers need to discuss ways of:

- **enabling large sibling groups to live together in care** e.g. by reviewing practice on removing siblings; by recording the location of all siblings that have been removed from a birth mother; by ensuring adequate support for foster carers who take sibling groups; or by allocating a suitable property to a large sibling group and finding foster carers to care for them.

- **removing restrictions** e.g. by engaging fully with other adoption agencies (rather than just seeking to place their own looked after children with their own approved adopters); ensuring there are enough funds to pay the inter-agency fee to other LAs or VAAs *(ASG 2.71)*; and ending automatic exclusions, e.g. for reasons of age, ethnicity, sexual orientation or health *(ASG 3.14)*.

- **encouraging foster carers to adopt a sibling group** e.g. by discussing the potential with foster carers and negotiating ongoing financial and social work support, if it is in the children's best interest to be adopted by their foster carers *(ASG 2.5–2.8 and 3.24)*.

- **minimising delay** by ensuring that large sibling groups are featured in family-finding magazines and placed on the Adoption Register as soon as possible. They could also make it easier for social workers to complete the necessary paperwork, e.g. by not viewing a sibling group as one case or by allocating two social workers to a large sibling group.

When siblings have to be separated

When siblings cannot all be fostered together, the social worker should discuss this with the children and, if possible, ensure that they are always placed with a sibling with whom they get on well and that they remain together (see Leathers, 2005 and ASG 4.12).

If potential kin carers want to separate siblings, it may be appropriate to discuss with them the importance of maintaining sibling relationships. The adverse effects of separation can be reduced by fostering siblings in the same area, enrolling them at the same school and facilitating frequent sibling contact. This provides reassurance for the children that their sibling relationships are valued and will be maintained.

8

Recruiting adopters for large sibling groups

RECRUITMENT METHODS

In our sample most adoption agencies used information packs, open evenings or information days, media interviews and various kinds of advertising to recruit adopters. However, most of their recruitment materials only mentioned siblings briefly. Here is a good example of how the needs of siblings to remain together were highlighted in an information pack:

> **One, two, three or more?**
>
> *Where possible, we try to keep brothers and sisters together and welcome applications from people with room in their lives to adopt more than one child.*
>
> *James, aged three, John, aged six and Mary, aged seven, have always lived together. Their parents abuse drugs and are unable to care for them. Mary often took over the role of her parents. The three children need to be together with adopters who are able to manage their insecurities and loss. This can be extremely challenging.*
>
> Extract from adoption information pack [LA 1]

Information provided by social workers or the media had made eight adopters (22%) decide to take a sibling group, because they believed passionately that it was wrong to separate siblings.

The adoption agencies did not advertise extensively due to the costs involved, but they found various ways of obtaining media coverage. Examples include: putting flyers about adoption in the payslip of every LA employee; involving a local celebrity, who had been adopted, in publicity; being interviewed, especially during National Adoption Week;

writing articles or letters to the editor; and organising a roadshow with sibling group adopters. Some adoption managers claimed that having a good reputation as an agency reduced the need for advertising.

Some agency staff stressed the importance of having a rolling programme of recruitment and welcoming applications. Accepting applications only from those who were willing to take older children or sibling groups had "decimated" recruitment in one LA and reduced the opportunity to discuss this possibility with other adopters. Giving "higher priority" to sibling group adopters was also not always effective.

Five sibling group adopters were initially rejected for the following reasons: the LA did not need any more adopters; had no children who could be placed with them; or did not want to place children with a same-sex couple, a member of the armed forces or those who wanted to adopt rather than having birth children. They all adopted through another agency but later one of the five adoptions partially disrupted with two children returning to care.

In some cases LAs may have to resist attempts by other professionals to turn down adopters who are willing to take a large sibling group. Our study included a case where a children's guardian had apparently recommended that four siblings should be split with two remaining in long-term foster care, because s/he thought it would be impossible to place them together for adoption, *even though approved adopters were waiting specifically for these children.*

When recruiting adopters for specific siblings, one LA manager recommended arranging mini in-house adoption exchanges and involving social workers. She said this could help to reduce delay because social workers could find out quickly if the potential adopters lived too close to the birth family.

Featuring a very large sibling group on television had also proved an effective way of finding potential adopters in a case described by a social worker:

> *When the group of five siblings was featured on television, over 200 people responded. Two social workers drew up a shortlist of 40, and they each identified five potential families before finally choosing one. The prospective adopters were assessed very quickly (within three months) because the children had been waiting a long time.*

The Adoption Register was much appreciated by all agencies because it enabled LA staff to locate approved adopters quickly for specific children. However, the inability or reluctance of some LAs to pay the inter-agency fee required for a VAA placement limited their use of the Adoption Register.

WHAT MAKES A DIFFERENCE?

The five LAs in our study emphasised the importance of having a social worker who really knows the children, providing very good information and offering an adoption allowance and support package to reassure potential sibling group adopters that they will be able to manage. One adoption manager commented:

I think now that we are able to advertise that an adoption allowance will be attached to this placement, I think that enables more people to come forward...And the availability of having a play specialist, a therapist. If parents are struggling with a child's behaviour...we can get (our) play specialist in quickly so they don't have to wait, and that's proved to be really useful. That is really a very good resource.

PRACTICE IMPLICATIONS

- **Our findings indicate the benefits of taking every opportunity to highlight the needs of siblings to remain together** by including short case studies or personal statements by siblings or their adopters in information packs, brochures and presentations. When talking to prospective adopters or the media about siblings, it can be crucial to emphasise the distress of siblings who are separated by adoption and the benefits of keeping them together.

- **Some adopters are willing and able to take large sibling groups, so it is a mistake to assume otherwise.** Instead, LAs need to find ways of making this seem possible and even enjoyable. The most effective way is probably to invite sibling group adopters to speak about their experiences at introductory sessions. Details of sibling groups should also be placed on the Adoption Register without delay and strenuous efforts made to find a suitable family.

- **Many applicants spend a long time thinking about adoption before contacting an agency, so a prompt response is essential** (ASG 3.14). It also helps to establish a rolling programme of recruitment, to encourage referrals from other agencies and to take enquiries from a wide geographical area. It is probably not a good idea to restrict applications to adopters willing to take particular categories of children or to make unduly onerous demands, such as requiring adopters to provide a separate bedroom for each child.

- **To widen the options for children and adopters, LAs need to engage fully with other adoption agencies through their local consortium.** There is no inherent reason why a same-sex couple, a member of the armed forces, or those who choose to adopt rather than having birth children should be regarded as unsuitable adopters, so their application should be considered (ASG 3.14). Extra support may be needed for a sibling group adopter whose partner is away for long periods of time.

- **Arranging mini in-house adoption exchanges** and involving social workers can be a good way of recruiting adopters for a specific sibling group. Adopters sometimes decide to take more children than they originally intended, when they see photographs and profiles of sibling groups. In-house exchanges can also help to reduce delay, but they should always be used in conjunction with other approaches.

- **A range of individualised material about each child – photographs, artwork, film-clips – can be presented at exchange events.** This helps adopters to appreciate the children's individual characters and needs. Using film footage is vital for disabled children, because disability can be presented as *part* of the child and not the whole story (Cousins, 2009).

9

Sibling group adopters' motivations and choice of agency

The majority (32) of the sibling group adopters chose to adopt due to infertility, but four couples (including a same-sex couple) chose to adopt rather than having birth children. A couple with older children who would soon be leaving home adopted because they wanted to do something worthwhile.

The vast majority (89%) of the adopters said they had wanted to adopt siblings right from the start. Most adopters were thinking in terms of two children, but some stated that they had always wanted a large family.

Half of the adopters had grown up in a sibling group themselves, but 40 per cent had grown up as an only child. Some relished the challenge of taking on so many children; others thought it would be easier to parent a sibling group than an only child.

HOW ADOPTION PRACTICE AFFECTED ADOPTERS' DECISIONS

It was clear that adoption procedures and practice could influence adopters' decisions to apply to adopt a sibling group. Just over half (51 per cent) of the adopters had concluded that going through the adoption approval process for a second time was to be avoided at all costs, and they had reached this decision as a direct result of their experiences. Here are two of their comments:

> Never again!

> It's a horrific … it's a huge process, and it is really draining and time-consuming, and … we wanted to get it all over and done with in one go.

Some adopters, who were initially thinking of adopting one child and then possibly taking another, changed their minds when they realised the complexity of the adoption process. Time was an issue especially for older adopters, as it is seen as good practice to wait for about two years before starting the adoption process again, and some older adopters felt that, if they wanted more than one child, they could not afford to wait. Interestingly, this situation may change with the Government's proposed adoption reforms, which include a radically redesigned two-stage training and assessment process in England:

> For the majority of prospective adopters the first stage (pre-qualification) will be completed within two months and the second (full assessment) within four. There will be a fast track process for people who have adopted before...
>
> An Adoption Action Plan: Tackling delay (DfE, 2012, Para 76)

WANTING TO KEEP SIBLINGS TOGETHER

Twenty-two per cent of the adopters (8) wanted a sibling group because they believed passionately that it was wrong to separate siblings. Listening to adopters talking about their experiences of taking a sibling group had led some to conclude: 'If other people can do it, then probably we can!' Some adopters had reached this decision specifically because a presentation by a social worker had spelt out the possibility of siblings being separated, while others were inspired by a heartbreaking story in the media or by reading and discussing profiles of large sibling groups in adoption magazines. Here are two of their comments:

> [The local authority] runs an introduction evening ... and we came away from that and independently had concluded and said to each other that we should offer for a sibling group of three. ... That was the moment, coming out of that evening, because they gave you scenarios, and one of the scenarios was this group of three being split up ... and that was it. We have never wavered from that.
>
> When you're reading the context and that, saying they could be split, and in my mind, I can't do that, not with children, you know what I mean? I want to keep them together! ... (Seeing a group of five siblings in Be My Parent) that's when I realised that I couldn't split a big sibling group up. Until then, I was happy with two...

One couple decided not only to adopt a large sibling group but also to choose older children, because they knew that older children were likely to be "passed over".

A BETTER CHANCE OF ADOPTING A BABY OR NOT WAITING SO LONG TO ADOPT

A quarter (nine) of the adopters had concluded that asking for a large sibling group would give them a better chance of being considered for younger children and/or becoming adopters more quickly. This included a parent, who viewed taking a sibling group as the only way of adopting white children in a London borough. Often their expectations were fulfilled, as can be seen in the following two statements by adopters:

I knew I would have a better chance of having a younger child as well as a three- or four-year-old and, of course, that's what happened, because (the youngest child) was only seven months old when they were placed with me.

Because we were prepared to take three children, we were in quite a lot of demand ... we had about six enquiries in a week.

However, adoption practices sometimes have unintended perverse consequences. For example, although adoption agencies often seek to place sibling pairs with younger adopters who are healthy and energetic enough to meet the children's needs, older adopters are sometimes considered for large sibling groups simply because the children are harder to place. This was reflected in the experience of one adopter:

When we realised that we were unlikely to get two children of a youngish age, we started to look at three ... While they were considering placing the three of them together, we were looked at quite favourably. As soon as they decided the children's needs were too great to place them together and they were going to split the group, they decided that we were too old to take the younger two who were five and three, but we would have been all right for the six-year-old girl.

PRACTICE IMPLICATIONS

- **Adoption staff should seek to recognise and encourage potential sibling group adopters** e.g. by arranging for them to hear from or talk to sibling group adopters (ASG 3.20). Discussions, presentations and media coverage of sibling groups being separated can also be crucial in motivating adopters to take on large sibling groups. There are people who are willing to do this.

- **Agency staff could make the adoption process more engaging, less repetitive and less time-consuming.** This would be in line with the Government's proposed adoption reforms which include a radically redesigned two-stage training and assessment process.

- **Social workers can ask prospective adopters whether they are likely to want more than one child** and, if so, they can discuss the pros and cons of adopting siblings or adopting children from different families consecutively.

Adopters raised in large families may regard it as natural for a family to consist of three or more children. Social workers need to explore the question of how many children each partner is likely to feel comfortable with, and the couple may need to reach a compromise.

- **Infertility is not the only valid reason for wanting to adopt**, and those who choose to adopt rather than having birth children should not be considered unsuitable for that reason.

SIBLING GROUP ADOPTERS' REASONS FOR CHOOSING THEIR ADOPTION AGENCY

The adopters gave many reasons for their choice of adoption agency, including location of the agency, the attitude and behaviour of staff, the publicity and profile of the agency on the internet, and recommendations by other adopters.

Two-thirds (25) of the sibling group adopters had approached an LA first to enquire about adoption, but five were rejected initially and a further three went elsewhere because LA staff did not respond quickly or they did not like their attitude. As a consequence, 20 of the adopters were approved by a VAA and only 17 by an LA. Five LA adopters did not realise they had a choice.

All the VAA adopters said they had chosen their adoption agency because they liked their attitude or approach, but this was the case for only 47 per cent of the LA adopters. However, one couple in our sample went to another agency after a VAA social worker was "scathing" about the viability of adopting a sibling group.

The adopters appreciated adoption social workers who are honest, friendly, professional, realistic and encouraging, and who responded promptly and allowed adopters to 'go at their own pace'. It was also reassuring for sibling group adopters to have a social worker who was experienced and knowledgeable. Those who made adopters feel patronised, pitied or undervalued were not likely to see them again.

Three adopters chose a VAA because they wanted an agency that was committed to finding the right children for them and were afraid that the LA might try to "offload" their looked after children onto them. Other reasons for not approaching an LA included the belief that they would be rejected because they were "the wrong colour" or "the wrong age".

The promise of "life-long" support was a key factor for those who chose a VAA.

> She said that they were used to placing larger groups and supporting people through that, and continuing the support as a life-long support. It wasn't once you'd done it, that was it and you were dumped. It was, 'If you need support, we'll always be there'...and they were on your side.

In one case it was clear that the LA was interested only in placing their own looked after children and had no wish to participate in recruiting adopters for children in other parts of the country.

PRACTICE IMPLICATIONS

- **First impressions are so important.** Does the agency respond quickly and positively when prospective adopters contact them initially? Adoption agencies could perhaps benefit by seeking feedback not only from those who use their services but also from those who contact them but do not return.

- **Attitude is also crucial.** Do agency staff appear welcoming, friendly, knowledgeable and professional? Do they show respect for prospective adopters and a desire to find the right children for them? Some LAs will need to work hard to reverse negative perceptions of the quality of their services – and some VAA staff may also need to examine their own attitudes to prospective sibling group adopters.

- **The offer of ongoing support can make all the difference.** When prospective adopters were thinking of taking on a large sibling group, it was very reassuring to have a VAA promising life-long support. LA staff need to consider how they can offer a similar assurance that continuing support will be provided, if it is needed.

- **It is vital that LAs do not focus solely on placing their own looked after children for adoption.** This approach inevitably reduces the choice for children and adopters in their area, and it can also mean that potential sibling group adopters are turned away. If LAs do not engage with other adoption agencies, there will always be a conflict of interest between trying to place looked after children and helping prospective adopters to find the right children for them (ASG 4.17). LAs which introduce restrictive criteria (see ASG 4.20) are not likely to be recommended by adopters.

10
Assessment

As assessing siblings for permanent placement has already been covered in a BAAF good practice guide (Lord and Borthwick, 2008), this chapter will focus almost entirely on the assessment of sibling group adopters. However, some comments are very relevant to the assessment of large sibling groups and are included here.

ASSESSING CHILDREN

In our study, adoption staff said that assessing each child in a sibling group and completing all the adoption forms for each child took a lot of time. If the LA's case management system recorded a sibling group as "one case", this created additional caseload pressure and a huge volume of paperwork for the social worker. They also acknowledged that children's social workers were also not always experienced in assessing sibling relationships and attachments.

ASSESSING ADOPTERS

There appeared to be very little specific training for social workers on assessing sibling group adopters and dealing with sibling group issues. Social workers had to learn by experience or from colleagues. Adoption managers attributed the confidence of their social work staff to experience in placing siblings for adoption. Some also emphasised that working in a team where such placements occurred regularly had led to increased confidence and optimism among all team members.

Some agencies used the same standard form and procedure for assessing all adopters, although nearly all the managers thought that additional areas needed to be considered with potential sibling group adopters.

The adoption service in one LA was being restructured so that adopters would no longer have a change of social worker after being approved.

Who might be a suitable sibling group adopter?

Adoption staff wanted to assess whether the adopters understood sibling group dynamics; could differentiate and meet the competing needs of individual children; had a good support network and experience in caring for children; could tolerate stress; and had realistic expectations. One LA manager commented:

> I think it would be about their experience of children and their confidence in managing a group of children who may have been treated differently in the family and may have had very different roles, and how they would manage different attachment behaviours within a wide age range. We just need to be sure that people can balance the different needs of children. We would want to ensure they had enough support in their lives, whether that was the community, friends or family.

Having a strong marital/partner relationship that had been "tried and tested" was seen as a crucial issue to assess. In particular, staff stressed the importance of adopters being united in their determination to adopt a sibling group and able to support each other through the difficulties. There was also an emphasis on practical considerations and whether one parent would be able to stay at home to provide the stability the children would need.

Conversely, adoption staff said applicants were unlikely to be considered for a sibling group if they were emotionally vulnerable, socially isolated, struggling financially, single or totally unrealistic. Age was not a barrier, but being fit and healthy was emphasised by some staff.

Social workers assessed the abilities of prospective adopters by discussing the needs of siblings featured in adoption magazines and by asking how they would deal with hypothetical situations. They also urged applicants to acquire childcare experience by doing voluntary work or by caring for the children of friends or relatives. In one agency, adopters were shown a short video of a family and then asked to talk about the children's interactions. A VAA manager commented:

> I think what we try to work out is those individuals who will feel comfortable with the sort of family life that comes with a larger sibling group – a noisy, more chaotic household – and who's going to think, 'That's really great and how family life should be' and who's going to think, 'I'm out of control here. This is horrendous. Get them out!'

Interestingly, another VAA manager refused to specify any crucial factors or desirable qualities for sibling group adopters on the grounds that adoption agencies should be enabling people to fulfil their potential, not looking for reasons to limit their eligibility. He wanted to know if the agency could make it possible for prospective adopters to take a large sibling group by providing appropriate support.

Adopters with birth children

Most adoption staff would not consider placing three or more siblings with adopters who had birth children living at home. This was because they believed it would be difficult to match children successfully; the impact on the birth children could be overwhelming; a sibling group would alter the family dynamics; and there would be an increased risk of disruption. However, one couple had successfully adopted two groups of four siblings with a large age gap between the groups. Their LA manager commented:

> It must be a family assessment, not just a couple assessment. You can make it fun. We do family projects with children to get them to talk about their family and themselves, what they are like, what it will be like to have more children in the family.

Financial security and family accommodation

LA managers were divided as to whether adopters needed to be financially secure and differed in the extent to which they were willing to provide financial support. Sometimes social workers seemed to assume that prospective sibling group adopters would have large enough accommodation already. However, this is a problematic assumption, particularly in London where the high price of property means that few would-be sibling group adopters had much spare space and often both parents had to work to meet their mortgage payments. This resulted in some sibling groups being placed far away from their home area, particularly from London. Nor was it easier when prospective adopters were living in social housing, as one VAA manager explained:

> Local authorities or housing associations will not re-house you until the children are in place. Even if you approve people, they won't move them until the children are placed, so what do you do? Place three children in a two-bedroom flat in the hope that they're going to be re-housed?...I can understand them not doing it before, but if the panel has agreed the match, why cannot the housing authority then look for a larger property for them?

Interestingly, the size of accommodation did not appear to be an issue for adopters working in the armed forces: we were told adoptive families in the forces could usually be moved to larger accommodation fairly easily.

Encouraging adopters to take a large sibling group

Most of the adoption agencies emphasised that they would not push any adopter to take more children than they wanted or would be able to manage. However, staff in seven VAAs and one LA said they often encouraged adopters to consider taking a sibling group and helped them to recognise that they had the ability to do this.

Adopters' perceptions

Assessment process did not focus on siblings

Just over a third of the adopters had announced right at the beginning of the assessment process that they wanted to adopt a sibling group. However, many of them thought their assessment had not focused on their capacity to parent a sibling group. Using a standard assessment process for all adopters and constantly referring to "the child" had sometimes given prospective sibling group adopters the impression that they were not being listened to. One adopter, however, described how the issue was addressed systematically throughout the assessment:

> *Because we'd always said we wanted three or four, I suppose it was just incorporated in the assessment all the way through. It wasn't, you know, tagged on as a last minute thing or one session or anything like that... so whenever you looked at any particular issue, it was with regards to having all those children and how you'd manage different sibling needs.*

Adopters' reasons for thinking they could manage a sibling group

The reasons that adopters gave for thinking that they could manage a large sibling group included experience in working with or caring for children; expecting to receive support from family and friends; having grown up in a large family; and having a strong relationship. Generally, the responses of VAA and LA adopters were very similar with one notable exception: 85 per cent of the VAA adopters thought that the support provided by their adoption agency would enable them to manage a sibling group, but only 41 per cent of the LA adopters felt confident of this.

Encouragement or pressure?

Adopters responded very differently to suggestions about increasing the number of children they were willing to adopt, and this depended very much on their adoption agency's approach. One couple who had been encouraged to take more children than they originally intended said they felt "really proud" when their social worker told them that she thought they could easily parent three children. They emphasised that there was no pressure, and they felt able to consider this because, crucially, there was a promise of life-long support. However, there is a fine line between encouragement, persuasion and pressure. In our study, five adopters had felt some pressure or persuasion to seek approval for more siblings than they had intended, and two of these placements partially disrupted with a total of three children returning to foster care.

One adoptive mother, who had been totally overwhelmed by the demands of the three siblings she and her husband adopted, described her social worker's approach:

> [The social worker] said, 'Okay, what are we looking for then?' And we said, 'Well, a boy and a girl under five,' and she said, 'Everybody wants that, you'll never get that ... and they're few and far between ... Okay, let's broaden your horizons a bit. Older? More?' We said, 'Well, we had wondered about three.' She said, 'Three, good! They'll snap your hands off with three. Jolly good! ... Okay, now you're not going to get three under five ... because of the age differences', and then we moved up to about [age] seven. So we said, 'Three under seven.' 'Lovely, sorted!' (laughter) ... It wasn't done in an undue way ... but yeah, possibly a bit over-persuaded.

Four adopters said they had felt pressurised by VAA staff, and in three cases this apparently happened just before the panel met to discuss their application. An adopter who had come very close to ending the placement expressed cynicism about the motivation of VAA staff:

> She came out and she looked around the house, and her comment was, 'Oh, it's a beautiful house for three!' ... They do the same amount of work for one, two or three children, but they get three times the amount of money ... and yes, for that reason we were pressurised into doing it. When we went to panel, we were still saying, you know, 'Really, two is where we want to be', but they put us forward for three, and of course, once we're approved for three, then that's it ... She completely, you know, discounted looking at two, completely. It was always three, so we were heavily pressurised by that stage.

PRACTICE IMPLICATIONS

- **Agencies with experience in placing large sibling groups should share their experiences and expertise.** The lack of available training on placing sibling groups for adoption suggests that there may be a "marketing opportunity" here for adoption agencies which have a lot of experience in placing sibling groups and are willing to share their expertise.

- **Continuity is very important, so it helps if the social worker who assesses the adopters also supports them during and after placement.**

- **There are people willing to take on the challenge of adopting a large sibling group.** Caring for three or more siblings will make huge demands on the adopters emotionally, physically and mentally, but there are people who have the determination and commitment to do this.

- **LAs could actively help adopters secure suitable accomodation.** Adoption staff are justifiably wary of placing sibling groups in families with birth children. However, risks can be reduced by fully involving birth children in the assessment and having an age gap of at least three years between the youngest birth child and the oldest adoptee (Wedge and Mantel, 1991).

- **Families who do not have a large enough home need not be turned away.** LAs may be able to place more sibling groups for adoption if they actively look for ways of enabling suitable adopters to have large enough accommodation, e.g. by paying for a loft conversion.

- **Social workers should respect an applicant's wish to adopt a sibling group.** When prospective adopters say they want to adopt three or more siblings, social workers should be willing to discuss what this will involve, rather than ignoring the issue or constantly referring to "the child" in the singular.

- **Social workers can enable adopters to recognise that they have the capacity to take three or more siblings**, perhaps because they know how to promote healthy family interactions or they are good at organising. However, "stretching" adopters' preferences may have very serious consequences (Farmer and Dance et al, 2010). Social workers should never try to persuade or pressurise prospective adopters to take more children than they want.

11

Preparation for adopting sibling groups

PREPARATION FOR ADOPTERS

All the adoption agencies provided initial preparation training for adopters, typically four days of training with intervals in between. Additional training for those who wanted to adopt a sibling group was not usually available. One VAA provided a one-day workshop for friends and relatives of the adopters to give them some understanding of the reasons behind the behaviour of looked after children.

Some adoption staff said they never shared children's profiles with unapproved adopters and others did so only to check how flexible the adopters were.

Sibling group adopters said they appreciated listening to adopters talking about their experiences. They also valued meeting adopters who already had a sibling group – but less than half of the agencies arranged such meetings.

Only 41 per cent of the adopters said that their preparation training was useful, but others appreciated aspects of the training, such as receiving information about looked after children; working on scenarios; discussing issues; exploring their own emotional responses; and meeting other prospective adopters. Some expressed concern that always presenting the "worst case scenario" could deter prospective adopters. Many adopters complained about a lack of practical information or strategies for coping with a sibling group and specifically the children whom they were going to adopt. Some adopters needed more information about attachment difficulties and how to respond to them.

PREPARING CHILDREN FOR ADOPTION

Adoption managers said that children's social workers were not always experienced in preparing children for adoption (as required by AAR 13 and ASG 2.17–2.21), and this work could be emotionally painful. However, the importance of preparing children is reflected in comments by two adopters, who said that the children did not know why they were being adopted and one child thought that her foster carers had died.

There were concerns about who would have the time to do this work and whether there was time for each child to be seen individually. One manager, whose LA had provided funding for a play specialist to do specific work on preparing sibling groups, explained:

> *If the children's social worker has not got the time to do that, which they often haven't, the adoption worker or the play specialist do specific preparation work for the move…I think sometimes it's presumed, because a sibling group have got each other…'Oh, they'll be okay, they've got each other', but it's different than what they've had. All children need to have direct work done with them to identify what their fears are and… help them process their own thoughts and fears individually.*

REUNITING SIBLINGS WHO HAVE BEEN SEPARATED

Adoption staff said it was difficult to re-unite siblings successfully if they had lived apart for a considerable time. (Almost half of the siblings in the study had been fostered separately.) However, some LA managers thought that these difficulties could be overcome, if regular contact was established quickly and increased before introductions:

> *You need to have sorted out the contact really at quite an early stage, and I think that helps to demonstrate to the children that you are going to be planning for them together. It also allows you to do the work together with them as a whole sibling group, which … is absolutely vital.*

In one LA, separated siblings had therapy to help them work through their feelings about the plan for adoption. This was because some siblings might not even be aware that they were related, and being brought together in a new adoptive home would often mean changes to their status and position within the family.

Adoption staff commented that putting all the siblings together in one foster home before introductions began could be fraught and arranging overnight stays appeared to be a better option. A VAA social worker described how this had worked with a group of five siblings:

With the five that I placed, because they hadn't lived together for quite a long time, we organised with one of the foster carers that she would have all of them, so they would wake up together and do all of those normal things together that they hadn't done. They were not moved but they went there for a weekend or overnight, so they could experience all the normal routines of living together, before moving in with the adopters.

Explaining the reasons for separation

Staff found it particularly painful to tell siblings they were going to be separated. They stressed the importance of being clear and finding the right words so that children would not get the wrong message (e.g. believing that the separation was because they were naughty or unattractive). One manager described a case where the explanation worked out with a psychotherapist was, 'The people who know you best think you need to live in different houses'. They also used ClipArt figures to represent the children and two different houses with a car moving between them to take the children for contact visits.

MULTI-AGENCY PREPARATION

Adoption staff said they liaised with schools and with medical and CAMHS professionals to ensure that the children and their adopters would not have to wait for specialist services. However, their responses indicated that most were thinking in terms of specific support for individual children rather than support for the siblings as a group.

Sometimes LAs organised a multi-agency meeting to ensure that the support plan would be implemented. Two managers also emphasised that Child Appreciation Days should always take place before a sibling group placement. One VAA manager thought that a series of formal or informal meetings was needed to seek the views of all the different professionals involved in a sibling group placement, including the foster carer, the family finder and 'whoever is responsible for agency finances'.

When children were being placed abroad (e.g. with a family in the armed forces), multi-agency work was complicated because agencies had to comply with the various requirements of service providers in different countries.

PRACTICE IMPLICATIONS

- **Developing a training session on adopting siblings** would be a good way of signalling the agency's commitment to keeping siblings together and may even attract prospective sibling group adopters. Training friends and relatives can help to increase the chances of adopters receiving appropriate and effective support from them, especially if the agency then involves key members of the adopters' support network in the adoption process.

- **Talks by sibling group adopters can inspire others.** Agencies can arrange for prospective adopters to discuss issues with sibling group adopters by setting up buddy schemes, organising private meetings or paying for membership of Adoption UK so they can use the message board.

- **Discussing children's profiles** is a good way of sharing information about the characteristics and needs of children waiting to be placed, and it helps prospective adopters to work out what matters to them most and what kind of children they would like.

- **Preparation training should include more information about attachment issues** and ways of helping children to feel more secure so that they can begin to trust their new parents.

- **Children's social workers may need guidance or support in explaining adoption to children and doing life story work**, as this can be emotionally painful. If children do not understand what is happening, they are unlikely to want to be adopted and this can threaten the stability of the placement.

- **It is essential that children know they are siblings before they are re-united.** Establishing regular contact is crucial, and arranging overnight stays in one foster home before placement can be helpful.

- **If siblings have to be separated, it is crucial that the reasons for this are explained clearly to the children**, perhaps using devices such as ClipArt, and that they are informed about plans for maintaining contact.

- **Multi-agency preparation is essential** to ensure that children and their adopters do not have to wait for specialist support to be provided. This is easier to organise when adoption agencies themselves employ therapists or educational psychologists and have good working relationships with external agencies. Organising Child Appreciation Days can be helpful. Specialist advice and support will be needed if children are being placed abroad, to help meet local requirements and policies.

12

Matching and providing information

LA adopters are usually matched with children from the same local authority or from an authority within their region. In contrast, VAA adopters are matched with children from all over the UK. These placements incur an inter-agency fee for the LA, so VAAs have to be more active in promoting their adopters. A third of the sibling group adopters were proactive in finding the children they wanted through adoption magazines. Six adopters thought they had been recruited for a specific sibling group, although this was not always made clear.

CHILDREN'S PHOTOGRAPHS

Adoption staff were wary of showing photographs of babies to potential sibling group adopters, in case they wanted the baby but were not really interested in the older siblings. The adopters were usually attracted by how the children looked in their photograph, and sometimes this persuaded them to take a large sibling group. A third chose children who resembled them. Some adopters said that information about the children's characters and activities (e.g. liking football) had helped them to feel a connection with the children.

LEARNING ABOUT THE CHILDREN

Adopters said the most helpful sources of information were foster carers, social workers and the child permanence and medical reports. Fourteen adopters (38%) had attended a Child Appreciation Day prior to placement, which gave them an opportunity to meet key people involved with the children and hear about their personalities and about what they had endured. All of them said this was helpful, and adopters found this a particularly positive experience when professionals clearly liked the children:

They organised especially for (us) a whole day where we met everyone, everyone who had been involved in their care...people who had known them and could tell us in person something about their history, and about their character, and about their nature...The really big thing about that was just how warm everyone felt towards them, and how much potential they felt that the children had, and how much they felt that investing in these children would really bring them on and make them wonderful adjusted adults.

One adoption manager stressed that it was important for the adopters to be accompanied by their own social worker to the Child Appreciation Day, because they could ask questions that might not occur to the adopters and check in advance if they would be able to meet professionals, such as the health visitor. Adopters expressed great appreciation for social workers who not only accompanied them but also took notes on each child and subsequently advised them on how the children were likely to behave and how best to respond.

However, there was concern that some professionals were unduly pessimistic about the children, and this might reduce the children's chances of being adopted.

PROVIDING ALL THE NECESSARY INFORMATION

Only 11 adopters (29%) were satisfied that they had received all the necessary information. A few thought they had been given a false impression of the children and said this made it harder to meet their needs. One adopter, who claimed that the child permanence report 'didn't suggest that anything was wrong at all', offered a possible explanation:

It's almost like, because the dogma is one should never criticise the birth family, social workers take this to the extreme and have sort of written out any potential criticism of the birth family from the paperwork which we've got. Well, unfortunately, that's going to leave us with quite a challenge when it comes to explaining to the children why they were taken away.

The adopters said they felt more confident about taking on a sibling group when their social worker was willing to discuss things, treated their concerns as valid and advised them on what sort of behaviour to expect from the children.

PRACTICE IMPLICATIONS

- **Adopters should not be steered in the direction of only one sibling group.** Nor should they be ruled out on the basis of marital status, age or ethnicity (ASG 4.5) or an LA's unwillingness to pay the inter-agency fee (ASG 4.19).

- **Discussing profiles in adoption magazines** can help adopters to develop their ideas about the kind of children they might want to adopt.

- **It is worth paying for good photographs of the siblings and including details of their characters and their likes and dislikes.** Our findings suggest that social workers should look for children who resemble the adopters or share their interests. They should not rule out all those who do not fit the adopters' stated preferences, because adopters are sometimes attracted to larger sibling groups than they previously intended.

  Adoption social workers have good reason to withhold photographs of babies when adopters are first being given information about a sibling group, but prospective adopters should not be expected to make their choice without seeing clear photos of the children (ASG 4.24).

- **Encouraging adopters to talk to foster carers beforehand** can build trust and provide vital information about the children's routines, likes, dislikes, etc.

- **Arranging a Child Appreciation Day** is an excellent way of giving the adopters a greater understanding of how the children have been affected by their experiences. This is crucial for sibling group adopters, and putting up large photos of each sibling makes it easier to discuss them individually. It is particularly helpful when social workers attend Child Appreciation Days with the adopters, make notes on each child and how they are likely to behave, and subsequently help the adopters to devise strategies for dealing with any attachment difficulties or behavioural problems.

- **It is important to provide adopters with all the necessary information**, even though in some cases social workers may not possess all the facts and adopters may not always take this in. Offering access to files helps to establish trust (ASG 4.24). Attempts to conceal information or delay its disclosure may undermine the placement or result in legal action. Prospective adopters want and need good quality information in good time about medical issues, sexual abuse, behavioural problems, the extent of any learning difficulties, and so on. There may well be gaps in what is known about the children's history and difficulties with predicting what might happen, but a failure to provide all relevant information about the children and their birth family will put LA staff in breach of their obligations under the Adoption Agencies Regulations 2005 (s17).

- **Professionals should not always offer the "worst case scenario", especially if they do not know the children well.**

- **Adopters need to be given a clear explanation about why the children were removed from their birth parents.** A failure to explain this clearly can lead to children concluding that they were mistakenly removed from a loving family. In these circumstances, continuing contact with the birth family may reinforce such beliefs and trigger difficult behaviour, which eventually undermines the adoption (Loxterkampe, 2009).

- **It is crucial for sibling group adopters to have a relationship with their social worker that is based on mutual respect.** Children also need to have a consistent and positive relationship with their social worker.

13

Introductions and placement

The aim of introductions is to get the children to the point where they are ready to go home with the adopters. This means having enough time and interaction with the adopters to build trust and overcome their fears (ASG 5.5). In our study the introductions lasted on average 10–14 days, sometimes longer for older children. When introductions took a week or less, the sibling group adopters said this was too short and overwhelming.

The adopters were introduced to all the siblings at the first meeting (even if they were living in separate foster homes), but the plan usually specified time to get to know each child individually. A VAA manager explained the reasons for this approach:

Where siblings have been fostered separately, they are always brought together for the first meeting…It's something about power and importance between the siblings, and you don't want to create a huge imbalance there. You want them all to be equally important in that first meeting.

ACCOMMODATION AND TRANSPORT

Many adopters had to travel great distances, especially if the children were living in separate foster homes. VAA adopters were significantly more likely to live many miles away from the local authority that was placing the children, in comparison with LA adopters who were more likely to adopt children from the same area. Unfortunately LA social workers did not always take account of the adopters' needs with regard to accommodation and travel when they were planning introductions as described in the following case study.

Case example

The three children were placed separately with three foster carers who did not live close together. The social worker did not know the children well and initially took the adopters to the wrong house. The adopters found a hotel but the LA said it was too expensive. As a result, they had to stay in Travelodges, which were booked up so they had to change hotels about four times during the two weeks of introductions. The adopters were expected to drive from one house to the next, doing bedtime and breakfast routines with each child individually. On the last day they had to drive to the three different foster homes to pick up the children, and they had to wait for the social worker, who was an hour late. Then they had to drive home (a five-hour journey). Their adoption social worker turned up to check how things were going within half an hour of their arriving home, and the adoptive mother commented, 'I could have happily bit her head off!'

Some adopters said trying to get to know a sibling group at a hotel was impossible. Others were grateful that the children's LA had arranged for self-contained accommodation to be provided for them:

The girls' local authority arranged for us to have a cottage...because it was January, cold weather, and it was wet and windy...and so we'd have a place to go back to that was comfortable for us all to relax and start to get to know the girls...That worked really well.

PREPARING CHILDREN TO MEET THEIR NEW PARENTS

Two families said they had faced major problems during and after introductions because the children had not been prepared and did not understand why they were being adopted or what was happening.

The crucial role of the foster carer

The adopters appreciated foster carers who welcomed them into their home; who were enthusiastic about the adoption and had prepared the children well; who explained the children's routines and each child's likes and dislikes; who let them have time alone with the children; who told the children that the adopters were mum and dad but quietly offered support; and who contained their emotions at the final handover.

The adopters also described various ways in which foster carers made the process easier for the children during transition by being positive about the adoption; playing the adopters' DVD; handing over the children willingly; inviting an adopter to stay overnight to care for a baby; or having other siblings to stay before the introductions. One adopter described the approach of a very experienced foster carer:

> She makes sure that when they come, you know, she's foster mum and she's helping them to find a new family, and she's looking after them and finding them someone nice, which is lovely. She said to the children, when ... we were taking them, you know, 'I told you I'd find you someone nice. Aren't they lovely?'

Although 86 per cent of adopters described the foster carer as helpful, a third had encountered some difficulties with foster carers who could not bear to part with the children. Tensions appeared to be inevitable when foster carers had wanted to keep the children and when children were securely attached to their carers or had been allowed or encouraged to call them mum and dad.

Reviewing the plan

Adopters appreciated a review of the plan, if the children's authority was willing to make changes to meet the needs of the children or to address issues, but many said they had no opportunity to discuss concerns.

PRACTICE IMPLICATIONS

- **It is helpful to introduce all the siblings simultaneously to the adopters**, as it makes it clear that they are all going to live together in one family, and this also helps to prevent jealousy or any suspicion of favouritism.

- **LAs can make the introductions easier by booking conveniently located self-catering accommodation for the adopters.** A large enough car with children's safety seats may also need to be hired if the adopters do not already have one.

- **It is the social worker's responsibility to prepare siblings for adoption, but foster carers can also help** by talking to the children positively about their new parents. Adopters will be delighted if the children call them mum and dad, but they may need help to understand a child who is more wary.

  When the plan is for siblings to be adopted together, it helps if the social worker tells the foster carers promptly and involves them in planning introductions (ASG 5.5).

- **Foster carers should be supported to prepare the child to move.** The final handover can be painful for foster carers who love the children and have cared for them long-term. They should have support from their social worker or an experienced carer to manage their sense of loss. Meeting the adopters before the introductions may be helpful, but social workers should pre-empt any possible attempt to sabotage the placement. If the foster carers can visit the children in their adoptive home or have regular contact, this may also be beneficial for them and for the children.

- **LAs need to be flexible** so that they can respond to the children's needs during the introductions. The review should take place halfway through the introductions, so there is time to deal with any concerns.

TRANSITION AND PLACEMENT

The start of the placement is likely to be easier if the transition from foster care to adoption is managed well. Most adoption managers said that, when planning the start of a placement, the following factors should be considered: children need time to settle in with their new parents before starting school; older children need time to say goodbye to friends; adopters may struggle to cope with siblings if there is too much unstructured time; and support services should be available. They said that, if possible, children should not miss school and should start at the beginning of term. In particular, they emphasised that nothing should be rushed and they recommended avoiding Christmas and not starting the placement on a Friday because support services would not be available at the weekend.

Adoption staff also said it was important for children to have an opportunity to explore their new home before the start of the placement. If a home visit was impossible, they thought it was crucial that the albums and DVDs prepared by the adopters contained lots of photos of their home. One social worker commented that the use of a webcam had been very helpful in one case.

Adoption managers agreed that having the foster carer bring the children to the adopters' home and then slowly withdraw could help to reduce anxiety and enable children to accept the transition to their new home. This approach meant that the children were less likely to feel that they were being taken away from, or abandoned by, someone they loved (the foster carer).

The adopters said they needed time to prepare their home for the siblings and to ensure that they had the necessary equipment and food that the children liked. A couple who were both working until the start date of the placement commented:

> Our turnaround time to get a non-child-friendly house ready for three children coming was two weeks! We had friends painting and parents

buying furniture ... I mean we were dead on our feet before the children arrived.

A few adopters reported that young children had been distressed by overnight stays before placement and did not understand why they had to return to the foster carer. In one case where the children stayed overnight in the temporary accommodation provided for the adopters, the adopters said the children were confused as to whether this was their new home.

WHICH WORKS BEST: PLACING SIBLINGS AT THE SAME TIME OR CONSECUTIVELY?

Adoption managers thought siblings should usually be placed at the same time to avoid jealousy, suspicions of favouritism or the establishment of a "pecking order". In most cases (92%) siblings were placed simultaneously, and most adopters thought this was a good decision.

Ten adopters (27%) insisted that it would not have worked if the siblings had been placed consecutively. They thought that being placed separately would have caused anxiety and distress, particularly in cases where one child (usually the oldest) had acted as parent to the others or they depended on each other for support.

In three cases siblings were placed consecutively for the following reasons: concern that the adopters would be overwhelmed by taking five siblings; wanting a separated child to establish herself and take on the role of a big sister when her younger siblings arrived a week later; thinking that the youngest child should be placed six weeks later because the siblings were in different foster homes. Only in the last case did this appear to be the wrong decision.

ACCEPTING THE ADOPTERS

Two-thirds (67%) of the adopters said that the children initially had difficulty in accepting them as their new parents. This was sometimes exacerbated when foster carers had encouraged children to call them "mummy" and "daddy" or did not allow the adopters to be directly involved in caring for children during introductions.

PRACTICE IMPLICATIONS

- **Some children may need more time to bond with their new parents** and this should be negotiated with the school or with a virtual school head (Berridge *et al*, 2009). Extra support may be needed if children are at home for a few weeks.

- **If children have depended on each other for support, separating them may cause anxiety and distress.** Consecutive placements can be helpful when one child or more has very difficult behaviour or when there is a big disparity in children's ages. Careful planning will be needed to ensure that siblings receive individual attention, especially when a baby is involved. For young children, it may be better to avoid overnight stays with adopters before placement.

- **There is no single "right" way of placing sibling groups.** The children's needs should determine how they are placed.

  Our findings suggest that it should not be assumed that siblings should be placed consecutively just because they have been living in separate foster homes.

- **Increasing contact and arranging overnight stays in one foster home is likely to be more helpful in preparing siblings for being reunited.** LAs should be willing to discuss problems and to change a plan which is clearly not working. Extra support may be needed.

- **Children should be helped to prepare for their move.** Children who are securely attached to their foster carer are likely to be bereft, and a child who has been "parenting" younger siblings may not regard an adopter as the person in charge. Foster carers can help to defuse these tensions by properly preparing children to move to a permanent family, being positive about the adopters, involving them fully in the children's care, and "letting go" of the child when it is time to move them on.

14
Providing support to sibling group adopters

Taking on three or more children is a huge commitment emotionally and financially, so sibling adopters are likely to need a substantial support package. Regular financial support can only be provided by local authorities. How can adoption agencies provide the right support and ensure that they are using their limited resources in the most effective way?

The main impression emerging from our study is one of inconsistent practice, not only between LAs and VAAs, but also within each sector. There were huge variations in the amount of financial, practical and emotional support offered to the sibling group adopters. This means that the opportunity to adopt or be adopted varies greatly from one area to the next.

Repeatedly, adoption managers mentioned the need to ensure that sibling group adopters had enough support, but it was also clear that most of them were assuming that much of this would be provided by the adopters' relatives and friends. This assumption was not always realistic.

Can we expect to see improved adoption support as part of the Government's adoption reforms? The expert working group advising the Department for Education made a number of proposals (below). The Government says it agrees in principle with the need to clarify and improve the consistency of adoption support but at the time of writing there is little indication as to whether these proposals will be implemented or not.

The Working Group has proposed an "adoption passport" – a transparent guarantee of the minimum support that adoptive families will receive. The passport would give prospective adopters greater clarity about what to expect, and it would ensure greater national consistency. As part of the minimum levels of support that the passport would guarantee, the Working Group proposes a series of possible extensions to existing adoption support. It argues that this would help recruit prospective adopters who are willing to adopt children with particularly complex needs. The Working Group thinks, for example, that there is a particular case for adopted children to have priority access to Child and Adolescent

Mental Health Services. The group suggests that adoptive parents should be given a voucher, entitling them to a parenting skills programme. It also proposes reforms to the tax and benefits system, suggesting, for example, that adoptive families should continue to be eligible for child benefit payments regardless of their income and that the tax credits system should be used to support those who adopt children with complex needs.

An Action Plan for Adoption: Tackling delay (DfE, 2012) Para 81

FINANCIAL SUPPORT AND ADOPTION ALLOWANCES

Most adopters rated financial support as the most essential support service. Nearly all the adopters (95%) in the study received a setting up allowance for furniture and essential equipment, but only 78 per cent received an adoption allowance. Of the eight families who did not receive an adoption allowance, one couple incurred debts and later refused to take another sibling. Three adopters were shocked when the LA did not pay the amount agreed, but two of them managed eventually to get that decision reversed.

Just under half of the adopters received a high enough allowance to enable one parent to stay at home. LA staff said they could not afford to provide this for all sibling group adopters, but most adopters viewed this support as essential. One adopter stated:

I could not have had these three children and had to work. It would have been impossible, so it (the adoption allowance) does provide an income of sorts to enable me to stay home and look after them.

VAA staff said LAs were increasingly reluctant to provide adoption allowances. They expressed concern that if the unwillingness to pay adoption allowances became widespread, only wealthy applicants would be able to consider taking a sibling group. Although some adoption managers said that their LA had occasionally paid for a house extension or a larger car, sibling group adopters were often expected to have a large enough home and car.

THE NEED FOR PRACTICAL AND EMOTIONAL SUPPORT

Meeting the physical and emotional needs of three or more newly placed children is complex and challenging. The scale and complexity of this task and the demands it makes on adopters were described as follows by a VAA manager:

Just the sheer impact of taking three kids is like giving birth to triplets then plus, plus, plus, plus, except you don't just feed, burp, change, play with them, put them back to sleep. You have all the other issues of older children struggling with coming to a new family, a new lifestyle, a new place; some being in school, and being terrified out of their tiny minds, and therefore reverting back to a lot of interesting behaviours, that may or may not have come out in the child permanence report.

Home help

Home help with household chores such as cleaning and laundry was provided for only 43 per cent of sibling group adopters, and this lessened the adopters' exhaustion and enabled them to spend more time with the children. VAA managers said it was difficult to get some LAs to recognise the need for home help, even when the adopters were struggling to cope. Adopters often emphasised the importance of having home help when they were dealing with difficult behaviour, frequent bedwetting or had three or more under-fives. One adopter who was trying to cope with all of this commented:

If it would have been offered, I would have bitten their hand off! … That's the one thing that really got me down was the amount of just the washing up, just the clothes and all the rest … It just felt like a mountain to climb every day with all that lot.

Two adopters commented that what they really needed was help in managing the children's behaviour as at the beginning they felt unable to go out with the children, even to the park, because they could not control them.

Social work support

Most of the support given to adopters came from social workers. Nearly twice as many VAA adopters said they had received emotional support from their social worker compared to LA adopters. Adopters appreciated social workers who made time to visit; helped adopters to understand the children's perspective; advocated on their behalf with other agencies, such as helping them to obtain a school or nursery place; and helped to devise strategies for managing challenging behaviour. They said it was also very helpful when the children's social worker could provide explanations for the children's behaviour.

Support from social workers with a good understanding of attachment issues was greatly appreciated by adopters who were struggling to form a relationship with their children or to understand the children's behaviour. One adopter commented:

[The social worker] knew all about attachment theory and she taught me quite a lot. That was … the first time that anyone had really ever

explained anything like that to me – you know, this is why they do it, this is what's happening.

Support from other adopters

Most adopters had attended an adoption support group set up by their agency. This support was valued by some but not by others. In particular, adopters appreciated opportunities to meet or talk to other sibling group adopters who were struggling with similar issues, as shown in the following comment:

> *Our agency are very good at putting us in touch with other adopters in the area ... particularly ones that have three or more and ones that still have issues going on – that are fresh rather than 'We've been doing it for five years and everything's fine'.*

Managing children's behaviour

Adoption staff thought that sibling group adopters would need help in managing the children's behaviour and group dynamics, but despite this, a third stated that such support was only provided sometimes. Lack of effective support in dealing with challenging behaviour and attachment difficulties appeared to cause the most distress to adopters. Some repeatedly emphasised the need for practical support and strategies to help them manage the children's behaviour. Others understandably felt they were being fobbed off, when they were told repeatedly that their child's disturbed behaviour was "normal". Five adopters were in dispute with the children's LA and were refusing to apply for an adoption order until support was provided to help them cope with the children's behavioural and attachment difficulties. However, there were also examples of good practice:

- Some agencies provided social work support in dealing with behavioural problems, and almost half of the adopters said that therapy had been provided for one or more of their children.

- Some agencies had social workers who had had specialist training in attachment issues and were able to help the adopters deal with difficult behaviour arising from attachment difficulties.

- Typical strategies focused on establishing daily routines and regular mealtimes to help the children to feel safe enough to trust their new parents.

- One adopter described being advised to use visual timetables that substitute pictures for words, with pictures for things such as breakfast, school, and going to the park or meeting grandparents. The children helped to put the timetable together by drawing the pictures and it was then hung on the fridge so everyone could see what was going to happen each day. This predictability was apparently very reassuring for a young boy with attachment difficulties.

Support with contact arrangements

All the LA respondents stated that sibling group adopters were likely to want support in managing contact arrangements, but this was not available for everyone (47 per cent received it, 38 per cent did not need it and 15 per cent said it was not provided.) See *Contact with siblings living elsewhere*, Chapter 16.

Respite care

LAs were reluctant to provide respite care and only did so in one case when it was already too late to prevent the placement from breaking down. Respite care was thought to be inappropriate especially at the start of a placement because, as one manager said, 'it has the feel of being like a looked after situation' with 'children being shipped around'. Five adopters who were exhausted by their children's difficult behaviour said they would have loved to have respite care but it had been refused or not offered. Here is one response:

> Turned down on the grounds that it would introduce another person into the children's lives, even though we were down on our knees...

Providing therapy

Almost half of the sibling group adopters said at least one of their children had received therapy and often this had "worked wonders". Indeed, for some a referral to CAMHS was viewed as a lifeline. They described quite a wide range of therapeutic treatments including play therapy, theraplay, one-to-one counselling, behavioural therapy, art therapy, occupational therapy and filial play therapy. Here is an adopter's description of a helpful therapeutic intervention with one of the most common problems – attention-seeking behaviour:

> She [oldest child] absolutely and totally just wants me to herself all the time, and ... she will go out of her way to get into trouble, because ... she's then getting my attention and (the other two children) aren't getting it. So we're in the process at the moment of doing mood and attitude charts at all times of the day ... We've got these forms which we're filling in, so she can sit down with the therapist and so she can reflect and think, 'Oh blimey!' ... She's taking a great interest in these forms, looking at all the boxes that mummy's been ticking on a daily basis, and ... the boxes I'm ticking are anger, rage, out of control. You know, most days at some point during the day she will experience those emotions ... but she's started getting better.

After building secure parent–child attachments, support may be needed to encourage healthy sibling relationships. Play therapy is one way of doing this. An adopter whose three children had benefited from play therapy commented:

> They needed to learn how to be a sibling group in a sense, so how to be together. [The oldest child] started going very much into this kind of mother role again and she would tell me, you know, 'It's time to feed [younger child] now.' … So the play therapy was there … to help them come together as a group and also to help [younger child] deal with the loss of the attachment to the foster parents … All the children [took part]. I didn't take part in it at all … They loved it; they still ask for it now. They had no idea it was therapy; they just thought it was play.

However, LA staff reported long waiting lists and problems in financing therapy. Only one LA adoption manager said that therapy was readily available in their area. Children with high SDQ scores did not always receive therapeutic support, and some adopters thought that CAMHS professionals did not understand attachment issues. The experience of two families also suggested that there was an acute lack of support services for children under age five with severe mental health problems.

Schools

Adopters appreciated social workers who helped them to obtain school places. Some had problems with staff in schools or nurseries who insisted that they should have put the children's names down months or years in advance despite current regulations giving looked after children priority in admissions.

Some adopters described how the ethos of a school and active intervention by teachers had supported them and improved the children's behaviour. Others complained that teachers had no understanding of adoption and blamed them for the children's bad behaviour instead of offering support. Sometimes there were long delays in providing learning support. An adoption manager also described how teachers could help to ease the children's transition to their adoptive home by organising a leaving party and inviting the adopters.

Responding to crises

Even adopters whose children were now happy and settled had sometimes experienced crises where the placement could have disrupted. In each case what was crucial was the way in which professionals had responded to the situation. Here is an example of an effective agency response:

> The adopters found it very difficult to manage the oldest child's attention-seeking behaviour at the same time as caring for a baby and a

two-year-old. After six months, the impact on their own relationship was so serious that, despite having been happily married for many years, they thought they were going to split up. The wife phoned their VAA and they responded immediately. The social worker, her manager and a post-adoption support worker visited. The adopters thought they were going to remove the children, but instead they provided some simple measures and strategies to support the adopters in dealing with the children's behaviour. It took the adopters about a year to work through these difficulties with the children, but the placement is now stable and happy. The wife remarked, 'It's like now looking back, why did we let it get to that stage? But at the time you just don't see that.'

Sometimes an adopter's sense of failure could be dispelled by a social worker who was willing to provide reassurance and affirmation. One adopter described how her social worker had saved the placement by saying 'a really helpful thing':

I remember saying to her one day … – and I was really worried about saying it – 'I don't think I love [child]. I don't love her because there is nothing there – I don't feel anything is happening.' And I fully expected them to say, 'Right, that's it. Let's end it.' But of course instead she said, 'Well, you may never love her, and she may never love you, but what you've got is you've given her sibling relationships.' And because she said that, that took the pressure off me and I was able subsequently to form a relationship – but if she had been … blaming and cold towards me about that, I'm not sure that the placement … would have lasted. In fact, I'm sure it wouldn't have done … I suddenly didn't have to feel like the worst mother in the universe because I couldn't love this poor little girl who had been through all these dreadful things … I thought, 'Oh yeah, actually she's getting quite a lot out of being here'.

While adoption social workers carry the main responsibility for supporting adopters, other professionals can also provide vital support in a crisis. In another case, it was the intervention of a teacher and the offer of support through the child's school which helped to prevent the placement from disrupting.

Post-adoption support

At the time of interview only 32 adopters had obtained an adoption order. There were few differences in the number or type of support services received by VAA and LA adopters after the adoption order was made. However, VAA adopters (82 per cent) continued to report far more emotional support from their agency than did the LA adopters (22 per cent) and this difference was statistically significant. LA adopters were three times more likely than VAA adopters to be dissatisfied with the amount of support they had received.

Some agencies offered an unusually wide range of continuing training and support. For example, one VAA provided an advanced Webster-Stratton parenting group, a group for parents of adolescents, a joint workshop for teachers and adopters on adoptive children in schools, and story stem assessments to adopters, which offered some insight into each child's view of family life.

PRACTICE IMPLICATIONS

- **The promise of life-long support can be invaluable.** Taking on an entire sibling group simultaneously, having to gain the trust and acceptance of each child while responding to the needs of children at different stages of development and coping with any emotional or behavioural problems is a huge undertaking. For many of the adopters in our study, this was something they were prepared to do only because of the promise of lifelong support from their VAA.

- **Clarifying the support package available, including any financial support, can be encouraging.** Stating on the children's profile that an adoption allowance will be provided, subject to a means test for the adopters, might encourage more people to consider taking a sibling group (see ASG 9.27 and ASR 8). Adoption social workers have a crucial role in negotiating the support package and should establish early in the process how much financial support the LA is willing to provide. Agency staff should also advise adopters about claiming child benefit. Reneging on an agreed support package is extremely bad practice and should never happen.

  The stability of a sibling group placement may depend on an adoption allowance to enable one parent to stay at home with the children. It is inequitable that such support should be available in some authorities and not in others.

  LA managers may view expenditure on house extensions or larger cars as excessive or unaffordable, but this needs to be compared with the cost of keeping the children in foster care (ASG 9.33). Perhaps more "joined-up" thinking across local authority services is called for.

- **No adopter should ever be denied essential support.** It is very worrying that five adopters refused to go ahead with the adoption because they saw this as the only way of forcing the children's LA to provide the necessary support.

- **Home help is a relatively inexpensive way of providing valuable practical support** for sibling group adopters. Ideally home help should be offered to every sibling group adopter during the first three months of placement or longer if necessary. Perhaps agencies could offer a non-means tested payment for home help, and this could be given to a relative or other helper to provide regular support.

- **Providing a crèche can enable adopters to attend an adoption support group.** Agencies can help adopters to meet and/or talk to other sibling group adopters by organising informal meetings, setting up a buddy scheme or paying for membership of Adoption UK.

- **Respite care may be needed when adopters cannot cope.** This might involve providing support during the day rather than overnight stays.

- **Adopted and looked after children are likely to suffer from attachment difficulties and trauma**, so CAMHS professionals need to know how to work with attachment issues and ensure that services are targeted at those in the greatest need. In some areas these specialist services already exist, but elsewhere they may need to be developed.

  Adoption agencies will be able to meet children's mental health needs and respond to crises more effectively if they employ a therapist or have a social worker with specialist training in attachment issues. Sometimes it may be quicker for adopters to approach their GP for a referral to CAMHS.

- **Schools can provide crucial support for children and their adopters.** Social workers should encourage this by explaining to school staff the behaviour of adopted children, offering training in responding to attachment difficulties and trauma, ensuring that children with mental health issues are referred to CAMHS and insisting they are assessed for a special educational needs statement, if necessary.

  Adopters said that agencies sometimes argued about responsibility for providing support. Social workers should liaise to ensure (for example) that transitional allowances for individual support in school are available from the start of the placement and that children moving to another area do not automatically go to the bottom of the waiting list for mental health services. CAMHS also have a responsibility to liaise with services in another area to ensure that moves go smoothly.

  Under the changes to the adoption system announced in England in 2012, adopted children will in future be given the highest priority in school admissions – as is already the case for looked after children under the Education (Admission of Looked After Children (England) Regulations 2006.

- **Some thought needs to be given to identifying adopters who are in serious difficulties** and where the stability of a placement may be threatened. This is because some adopters are reluctant to ask for help in case they are perceived as failing or for fear that the LA may take the children away. When it is clear that sibling group adopters are struggling, agencies need to be ready to respond promptly, generously and effectively by assessing the type and level of support that needs to be provided and ensuring that they are.

15
The well-being of the children and their adopters

The adopters all completed a Strengths and Difficulties Questionnaire (SDQ) for each child who was aged 4–15 (a total of 109 children). All of them also completed a General Health Questionnaire (GHQ) on their own current mental state. In addition to these standardised measures, immediately after interviewing the adopters the researcher rated the stability of each placement and the warmth with which the adopters had spoken about each child. The key findings from these measures are as follows:

- Over a third of the 109 children scored within the abnormal range on the SDQ and 81 per cent of families had at least one child with an abnormal score. This is higher than would be expected in the general population but lower than in samples of looked after children. The main difficulty for all age groups was peer relationships. The older the child, the more likely the SDQ score was to be high.

- Fifty-four per cent of adopters scored within the normal range of the General Health Questionnaire (GHQ), but 35 per cent attributed their poor mental health (anxiety and depression) to the stresses and strains of being an adopter. Not surprisingly, the children's SDQ scores were correlated with the adopters' GHQ scores. One adopter wrote:

  I had been a teacher … before this. None of this prepared me for the "full on" emotional ride that three young children bring. My weight has gone up and down, my sleep habits have changed and my need for adult companionship increased. I am permanently tired even when they are at school.

- Nine families (almost a quarter) were struggling. The number of siblings with difficulties (rather than the severity of an individual child's difficulties) was associated with the placement being rated as having major difficulties.

- The warmth expressed by the adopters when speaking about the children was rated as high for 79 per cent of children and moderately high for 13 per cent of children. It was noticeable that the low warmth ratings were nearly all recorded in respect of the first and second child (the older children) in the sibling groups. However, there was no statistical association between children with high SDQ scores and lower parental warmth ratings. Some adopters are able to express warmth and commitment to the children irrespective of their emotional and behavioural difficulties.

PRACTICE IMPLICATIONS

- **Adopters need to be adequately prepared and supported.** Our findings suggest that it might be helpful if social workers use the SDQs completed by foster carers to plan adoption support and to prepare the adopters for the children's likely behaviours.

- **Adoption staff could consider ways of helping children to make friends and sustain relationships.**

- **Additionally, older children are likely to need more help and some children will need long-term support.** When sibling group adopters have a child who continually demands attention with challenging behaviour, a range of support (including therapeutic support) will be needed to ensure that the adopters can meet the needs of all the siblings.

- **When more than one child is assessed as having significant difficulties, a considerable amount of support (including therapeutic support) will be urgently needed to ensure the stability of the placement.** In urgent cases support can be provided without lengthy procedures (ASR 21).

- **Worried adopters may need practical or therapeutic support** to help them manage the children's behaviour. Emotional support is also crucial, as adopters may need reassurance that they are "good enough" parents.

When adopters do not express warmth when discussing a child, social workers should regard this as a red alert indicating the need for intensive support or intervention.

16
Contact with siblings living elsewhere

Many of the children in our sample came from very large families, and most (76%) had full or half-siblings living elsewhere. Arrangements were often made to maintain or establish contact with these children.

THE NEED FOR INFORMATION ABOUT SIBLINGS

Only about half the adopters said they had received a good explanation of why other siblings had not been placed with them. Nearly a third of the siblings living elsewhere were half-siblings, and there did not appear to be the same emphasis on maintaining contact with half-siblings as there was with full siblings.

Many adopters said it was difficult to explain about other siblings, if children were too young to understand or cope with the information. Some children wanted to know whether another baby would be allowed to stay with the birth mother, and the answer was not always clear.

Contact

Some adopters disliked contact (especially if they thought it affected children adversely), but others wanted 'to keep the door open' in case their children decided in the future that they wanted to meet their other siblings. About two-thirds of the sibling group adopters initially received support in dealing with contact (usually letterbox contact), and almost half of those who obtained an adoption order said they were still receiving help with contact. For a few families, the support had been essential in maintaining face-to-face contact with other siblings who were living with a birth parent. Two adopters were unhappy about being expected to manage contact visits involving birth relatives and siblings, as in the following response:

I am concerned about having to manage the contact ourselves from this year. I think it's essential for the children's social worker to be there to manage (the birth relatives), because otherwise we will have to take on the social worker's role and manage them as well as looking after the children – and I'm not sure I'm prepared to do that.

Adopters thought that contact had less meaning for younger children, who often did not recognise their siblings. Children in the same sibling group had different responses to contact, and this could make contact visits difficult for the adopters to manage.

Adopting another sibling

Five families had been approached about taking another sibling, but only one family (who had received generous support) felt able to do this.

PRACTICE IMPLICATIONS

- **Sooner or later children are likely to want to know about their other siblings,** so it is important that information about their circumstances and their whereabouts is recorded and shared with the adopters.

- **When siblings are separated, plans should be made for maintaining contact (ASG 7.11).** Children themselves do not distinguish between full and half-siblings. What is likely to be more important is whether they have lived with the sibling before. Children may also be keen to meet a new baby brother or sister.

- **Sharing information with siblings of different ages is complicated** as information needs to be age-appropriate for each child. Children who have been abused or neglected may be worried about the safety of other siblings, and may need reassurance or contact to allay their fears. They may also just want to know what their siblings look like.

- **Contact is not always beneficial for children** and their wishes and feelings should be taken into account (AAR 13). However, it may become important for children to meet and get to know their siblings at some later stage. As contact visits and letters can give rise to all sort of different emotions, each sibling may need to be encouraged to express how they feel about seeing their siblings, and each child's feelings should be taken into account.

- **Support with contact is important,** because it can be difficult to know what to write or say. Supervision is essential when direct contact with siblings involves birth relatives, and adopters should not be expected to manage visits involving birth relatives without support (see AAR 35 and 36).

- **LAs need to make it possible for adopters to take another sibling.** Sibling group adopters who have not received adequate support are unlikely to agree to take another sibling, and this means brothers and sisters being denied the opportunity to grow up together.

17

Adopters' perspectives on how it was working out

According to their adopters, the vast majority of the children adopted in sibling groups in our study were making progress and doing quite well or very well. Many adopters described their children as "blossoming" and said their more severe behaviours were reducing or had stopped. However, two of the adoptions had partially disrupted and two children in one family and one in the other had returned to foster care. The adopters in both cases stated that they had not received the necessary support to enable them to deal with the children's emotional and behavioural problems.

Becoming adopters of a sibling group had transformed the lives of the adopters. Not surprisingly, most adopters (68%) reported some difficulties. However, it is important to note that almost a third of the adopters (12) reported no difficulties or only a few minor problems. One adopter commented:

> Obviously it's a massive life change and experience, but we love the kids to bits, can't imagine life without them and the last year has just gone so quickly...Absolutely no regrets at all.

One of the most interesting findings in our study was that the responses from the six adopters who had taken sibling groups of four were particularly positive: half said they had had no difficulties and only one reported major problems, which were with the school and not the children. This echoes positive findings about very large sibling groups and their adopters in two other studies (Smith et al, 2006; Glidden et al, 2000) but the reasons for these findings are unclear. In our study, most of the children in sibling groups of four had low SDQ (Strengths and Difficulties Questionnaire) scores, but four children (in three sibling groups) had difficulties that interfered "quite a lot" with their home life, their friendships or their classroom learning. The positive responses probably reflect the outlook of the adopters as much as the behaviour of the children, because all of these adopters expressed high warmth towards all of their children.

Another significant finding was that, despite adopting older children, fewer voluntary adoption agency (VAA) adopters reported major problems. This may be due to the support they received, as VAA adopters expressed greater satisfaction than LA adopters with regard to support services.

SOME OF THE DIFFICULTIES

The behaviours identified as most difficult by the sibling group adopters in our study were attention-seeking and challenging behaviour, attachment difficulties and "parentification" – when a child had effectively assumed the role of parent to his or her brothers and sisters. Challenging behaviours included violence, self-harm, stealing and lying, and some adopters were also concerned about low self-esteem, soiling and bedwetting.

Generally, about half of the children quarrelled constantly (usually low level bickering) but they were also very close to each other and spent a lot of time together. Adopters often emphasised the siblings' sense of belonging to each other and viewed this as a source of comfort and support, as in the following statement:

> It's low-level continual fighting. We have stopped the physical violence now. The weird thing is they actually all really have a strong bond. They all really miss each other and love each other, and their fighting is almost like an interaction.

Six adopters had difficulty with "parentified" children. These children – usually the oldest – were often reluctant to relinquish responsibility for caring for their siblings, and this resulted in power struggles with the adopters. One adopter described the strategy she used to persuade her eldest daughter that she could safely hand over the care of her younger siblings:

> We have to, kind of, do it in a way that – 'Right, you show me how you do it and I'll follow you.' And that way she backed off, because she thought I was doing it the right way, and obviously we made a few changes along the way, and after a matter of probably three or four weeks she gave up anyway. She was too busy playing and enjoying herself ... But it was getting her to show me how to do it; it was her idea.

It was not unusual to have one child in a sibling group who continually demanded attention with very challenging behaviour, making it difficult for adopters to meet the needs of all the children in the family. Some adopters also found the children's behaviour hard to understand, if they had not received any specialist support in dealing with attachment difficulties – and five adopters were refusing to apply for an adoption order for this reason. This is perhaps an inevitable outcome of allowing LAs discretion in whether or not they provide the support assessed as necessary for individual adoptive families.

HOW WERE THE ADOPTERS COPING?

Some sibling group adopters said it was the hardest thing they had ever done, while others said everything 'just felt so right'. A third of the adopters were always tired, and a quarter said that having the children had put a strain on their relationship.

Surprisingly, coping with the actual number of children was rarely mentioned as a problem. One adopter of four siblings commented that it was just a question of getting used to buying 24 pints of milk at a time. However, caring for three or more children under school age was certainly not easy, and adopters who had to parent a sibling group for long periods on their own had also sometimes found this overwhelming.

About half of both LA and VAA adopters stated that their agency had helped them to resolve any difficulties they had had since the children were placed.

The wider family

Almost two-thirds of adopters said that their relatives had responded positively to the children and accepted them as part of the family, but in about 30 per cent of cases there were tensions with extended family members. Tensions often arose when relatives were worried about the adopters' ability to cope with the children's behaviour.

About half of the adopters said that the most helpful support during the adoption process had been provided by their own social worker or adoption agency. Surprisingly, only four adopters said that friends and relatives had been very helpful, but that may have been because the main focus of the study was on agency practice.

What made things harder?

Almost half the adopters complained about delays, bureaucracy and form-filling. Other problems included pessimistic social workers, being "fobbed off", conflicting reports, the failure to provide life story books and LAs' reluctance to accept responsibility for providing support. One adopter was adamant that delays could have been avoided by better organisation:

> The bureaucracy – dealing with the paperwork and meetings was a complete and utter shambles, and we were just pulling our hair out, because it just seemed to us that ... we were never going to get them home ... A meeting in [the children's LA] was postponed because the foster carers couldn't go, and they didn't hold it again for another 12 weeks. No babysitter was offered to help look after the children, so the foster carer could go to the meeting ... The reason the foster carer didn't

come down here was that nobody paid for her to come. They should get that sorted.

KEEPING THE SIBLING GROUP TOGETHER: RIGHT OR WRONG?

Most adopters (81%) believed it was the right decision to place the siblings together. Many emphasised how close the siblings were and how they had always been "the only constant" in each other's lives. One adopter expressed this in the following terms:

> *They have a unique bond, they have a common life experience, they have memories that only they can have and only they can share with each other. And it gives them strength, it gives them security, and it gives them a sense of being and it's their identity.*

However, four adopters were not sure and three adopters (including the two disruption cases) said it was a big mistake. When adopters expressed uncertain or negative views, it was usually because they thought that a child with severe difficulties needed to be an only child receiving one-to-one attention.

Almost two-thirds (65%) of the adopters said they would recommend adopting a sibling group to others, and some had already done so.

A NATIONAL ADOPTION SCHEME OR GATEWAY

We asked adopters for their suggestions on improving the service. One adopter, who had successfully adopted four siblings after being turned down by her own LA, suggested that one way of ensuring this did not happen to other potential adopters would be to introduce a national adoption scheme. She emphasised that this would help to establish a consistent standard of service:

> *I think there are people like us out there who are able to do it, but the system just knocks them back. The fighting they have to do to get things. I would like to see... I think the idea has been mooted by Adoption UK about having a national adoption scheme so you don't get local authorities who have many different agendas, different budgets, different priorities...If you had a national organisation, you wouldn't have places like (LA) saying to me, 'We don't need any more adopters'...Presumably a national scheme would say, 'We're taking on anybody that wants to adopt and nationally we must be able to find a child to match that'.*

A similar suggestion for a new "national gateway" was put forward by the expert working group advising the Department for Education on adoption reform.

> *The Working Group's second key proposal is the creation of a new national gateway to the adoption system. This would complement adoption agencies by providing a central point of contact for anyone interested in adoption. Through a telephone helpline and website, it would provide independent advice and information about adoption and how to apply to become an adopter. In particular, it would make sure those interested in adoption knew they were not obliged to adopt through their local authority, and help them to choose the right agency for them in their local area. It would also assess management information about how prospective adopters are treated and support a national customer service charter.*
>
> *We think the proposal for a new national gateway could dramatically improve the experience of those who enquire about adoption...*
>
> *An Action Plan for Adoption: Tackling delay* (DfE, 2012) Paras 79 and 80

The proposal was embraced wholeheartedly, and the new service, First4Adoption, was launched in early 2013.

PRACTICE IMPLICATIONS

- **Both conflict and closeness are to be expected when siblings are born in rapid succession.** Siblings are likely to benefit from being placed together, but practical or therapeutic support may be needed to reduce conflict and improve sibling relationships.

- **Adopting a large sibling group can be a positive experience.** It is also exhausting, particularly when all the children are under five and need a lot of physical care. Social workers need to assess whether prospective sibling group adopters have sufficient energy and are united in their determination to do this *with appropriate support.*

- **Post-adoption support is essential.** Extra support should be offered to any sibling group adopter whose partner is absent for long periods. Social workers can help to defuse tensions with the wider family by ensuring that appropriate support is provided. If relatives are to provide substantial support for sibling group adopters, it is crucial that they understand the experiences and needs of looked after children. Providing a workshop for relatives may help to bring this about.

- **The adoption process needs to be rigorous, but adoption teams should discuss ways of reducing delays and repetition.**

- **Professionals should not seek to avoid responsibility for providing support.**

18
Conclusions

Most of the sibling group adopters in the study reported positive outcomes for the children. These responses suggest that it is indeed possible to place large sibling groups for adoption successfully. Adoption staff who think this is impossible do a great disservice to the siblings in their care.

Often there seemed to be an assumption that taking three or more siblings would destabilise the placement, but our research showed that the adopters who experienced the greatest difficulties were not those who took larger sibling groups but those who had two or more children with serious behavioural problems.

We hope that our research may help to convince sceptical social workers, managers and individual professionals that they can actually place large sibling groups for adoption and that, with appropriate support, these placements can work well.

It is often considered difficult to find adopters who will take three or more siblings, but our study found that at least some of these difficulties were created by LA policies and the beliefs of individual professionals. LAs need to be willing to consider a wider range of people as prospective sibling group adopters and should not rule out, for example, VAA placements, applicants working in the armed forces or those who have other children (although a three-year age gap and careful preparation of the whole family are of course vital).

LAs need to view adoption as an inter-agency activity. Without this approach, some prospective adopters will inevitably be turned away and might never adopt. While so many children are waiting for adoption and when the personal, social and financial costs of keeping children in the care system are so high, it is unacceptable that LAs should squander the goodwill of prospective adopters in this way.

Many examples of good practice and effective support did not involve excessive expenditure. Often what was critical was an understanding of the children's needs, careful planning and preparation to ease the adoption process, a willingness to be flexible and an ability to respond quickly and appropriately when adopters were struggling to cope. The attitude and approach of social workers and their adoption agency are key factors.

However, it is also essential that LAs should have enough funds to pay the interagency fee, to provide adoption allowances and to offer therapeutic support for troubled children. If LAs become more reluctant to provide adoption allowances, we risk a situation developing in which only wealthy applicants can adopt large sibling groups. That means that children's chances of being adopted with their siblings will diminish and the costs of keeping them in care will increase.

It is worrying that many sibling group adopters said they had to fight to obtain the necessary support for their children and five were refusing to apply for the adoption order for this reason. This too is unacceptable. Sometimes these difficulties were due to social workers not having the necessary expertise, but adopters also spoke about budget constraints and agencies arguing about responsibility for providing services. It should be noted that the huge variation in the standard of service and support offered by adoption agencies in our study is made possible by a "let out" clause in the statutory guidance (ASG 9.6). All these issues need to be addressed, if adoptive families are to be given the support they need and deserve.

The findings of our study suggest that people who are willing to adopt three or more siblings tend to have remarkable determination, commitment and generosity of spirit. They also represent the best chance of securing a better future for many sibling groups who are in the care system waiting for a new family. These adopters should be valued, encouraged and given all the support they need, particularly in the first year of placement.

References

Avery RJ and Butler JS (2001) 'Timeliness in the adoptive placement of photolisted children: the New York State Blue Books', *Adoption Quarterly*, 4:4, pp. 19–46

Bank S and Kahn M (1982) *The Sibling Bond*, New York, NY: Basic Books

Berridge D, Henry L, Jackson S and Turney D (2009) *Looked After and Learning: Evaluation of the Virtual School Head Pilot*, Research Report DCSF – RR144, London: DCSF

BAAF (2007) *Chief Executive's Report*, 17/5/07, London: BAAF

Boer F, Verluis-den Bieman HJM, Frank MS and Verhulst MD (1994) 'International adoption of children with siblings: behavioural outcomes', *American Journal of Orthopsychiatry*, 64:2, pp. 252–262

Boneh C (1979) *Disruptions in Adoptive Placements: A research study*, Boston, MA: Massachusetts Department of Public Welfare

Buhrmester D and Furman W (1990) 'Perceptions of sibling relationships during middle childhood and adolescence', *Child Development*, 61:5, pp. 1387–1398

Child Welfare Information Gateway (2013) *Sibling Issues in Foster Care And Adoption*, Washington, DC: US Department of Health and Human Services, Children's Bureau

Cousins J (2009) 'Disability: still taboo in family placement?', *Adoption & Fostering*, 33:2, pp. 54–65

Dance C, Ouwejan D, Beecham J and Farmer E (2010) *Linking and Matching: A survey of adoption agency practice in England and Wales*, London: BAAF

Department for Education (2010) *Statistical First Release 2009–2010*, London: DfE

Department for Education (2011) *Adoption Statutory Guidance, Adoption and Children Act 2002, first revision February 2011*, London: DfE

Department for Education (2012) *An Action Plan for Adoption: Tackling delay*, London: DfE, available at: www.education.gov.uk/childrenandyoungpeople/families/adoption/a00205069/action-plan-for-adoption-tackling-delay

Dunn J (1984) *Sisters and Brothers (The Developing Child)*, Waukegan, IL: Fontana Press

Dunn J (1993) *Young Children's Close Relationships: Beyond attachment*, Thousand Oaks, CA: Sage

Edwards R, Hadfield L, Lucey H and Mauthner M (2006) *Sibling Identity and Relationships: Sisters and brothers*, Abingdon: Routledge

Farmer E and Dance C with Beecham J, Bonin E and Ouwejan D (2010) *An Investigation of Family Finding and Matching in Adoption: Briefing paper for the Department for Education*, DFE-RBX-10-05, London: DfE

Fratter J, Rowe J, Sapsford D and Thoburn J (1991) *Permanent Family Placement: A decade of experience*, London: BAAF

Furman W and Buhrmester D (1985) 'Children's perceptions of the qualities of sibling relationships', *Child Development*, 56, pp. 448–461

Glidden LM, Flaherty EM and McGlone AP (2000) 'Is more too many?', *Adoption Quarterly*, 4:1, pp. 67–80

Hegar RL (2005) 'Sibling placement in foster care and adoption: an overview of international research', *Children and Youth Services Review*, 27:7, pp. 717–39

Hughes D (2010) 'Expert paper 15 – LAC 8.4a, Siblings in care', as part of PH28, *Looked-After Children: Supporting evidence*, NICE, available at: www.nice.org.uk/guidance/index.jsp?action=download&o=47439

Ivaldi G (2000) *Surveying Adoption: A comprehensive analysis of local authority adoptions 1998–1999*, London: BAAF

Kim JY, McHale SM, Osgood DW and Crouter AC (2006) 'Longitudinal course and family correlates of sibling relationships from childhood through adolescence', *Child Development*, 77:6, pp. 1746–1761

Kosonen M (1996) 'Maintaining sibling relationships: neglected dimension in child care practice', *British Journal of Social Work*, 26, pp. 809–822

Leathers SJ (2005) 'Separation from siblings: associations with placement adaptation and outcomes among adolescents in long-term foster care', *Children and Youth Services Review*, 27, pp. 793–819

Lord J and Borthwick S (2008) *Together or Apart? Assessing brothers and sisters for permanent placement*, London: BAAF

Loxterkamp L (2009) 'Contact and truth: the unfolding predicament in adoption and fostering', *Child Psychology and Psychiatry*, 14, pp. 423–435

McKay S (2010) *The Effects of Twins and Multiple Births on Families and their Living Standards*, Birmingham: University of Birmingham

McRoy RG (1999) *Special Needs Adoption*, New York, NY: Garland Publishing

Mullender A and Kearn S (1997) *"I'm Here Waiting" – Birth relatives' views on Part II of the Adoption Contact Register for England and Wales*, London: BAAF

Quinton D, Rushton A, Dance C and Mayes D (1998) *Joining New Families: A study of adoption and fostering in middle childhood*, Chichester: John Wiley and Sons Ltd

Rosenthal JA, Schmidt D and Conner J (1988) 'Predictors of special needs adoption disruption: an exploratory study', *Children and Youth Services Review*, 10:2, pp. 101–117

Rushton A, Dance C, Quinton D and Mayes D (2001) *Siblings in Late Permanent Placements*, London: BAAF

Selwyn J, Sempik J, Thurston P and Wijedasa D (2009) *Adoption and the Inter-Agency Fee*, report for the DCSF by the Universities of Bristol and Loughborough, London: DCSF

Selwyn J, Sturgess W, Quinton D and Baxter C (2006) *Costs and Outcomes of Non-Infant Adoptions*, London: BAAF

Smith SL, Howard JA, Garnier PC and Ryan SD (2006) 'Where are we now? A post-ASFA examination of adoption disruption', *Adoption Quarterly*, 9:4, pp. 19–44

Triseliotis J (2002) 'Long-term foster care or adoption? The evidence examined', *Child and Family Social Work*, 7:1, pp. 23–33

Triseliotis J, Feast J and Kyle F (2005) *The Adoption Triangle Revisited: A study of adoption, search and reunion experiences*, London: BAAF

Wedge P and Mantel G (1991) *Sibling Groups and Social Work: A study of children referred for permanent substitute family placement*, Aldershot: Avebury Academic Publishing Group